TRENDSETTER REVIEW FOR THE FLAT

by Andrew Ayres

Raceform Limited

Compton, Newbury, Berkshire RG20 6NL

Tel: 01635 578080 Fax: 01635 578101

Web: www.raceform.co.uk

Email:raceform@raceform.co.uk

Printed and bound in Great Britain by Nuffield Press Limited

ISBN 1-901100-17-0

Introduction

The dictionary definition of statistics reads thus: numerical facts systematically collected on a subject. If any sport is given to such a study then surely it is horse racing.

Here, where we have detailed form, age, weight, draw, betting and trainer records to draw upon, there is a wealth of information hiding beneath the surface of each and every event.

Of course, uncovering that information is both demanding and time consuming. This book, which is an extension of the Trendsetters Guide that has appeared in the Raceform Update for the past 10 years, provides a solution to the problem.

In short, the spadework has been done and the relevant statistics prepared for your immediate use.

Our study takes in all home based Group One and Two races, alongside the major handicaps and selected events from overseas. We have included all 24 races from Royal Ascot, bringing the total number of contests covered to 111.

So how are the statistics used to best effect?

It can be tempting to find a fancied runner and then force it to fit the statistics on offer. This is to place the cart before the horse.

The results of our analysis must be used without bias. If your selection is a high weight but high weights have a poor ten-season record, think again. Read through the statistics available and cross off any runner that fails to meet our requirements. Let the trend be your friend!

Commonsense must also be applied. For example, if the statistics point toward a soft ground specialist and it hasn't rained for a month, you must look elsewhere for a potential winner. By using this open-minded but sensible approach, statistics can, and will, work for you.

ANDREW AYRES
JANUARY 2000

DONCASTER, SATURDAY MARCH 25
LINCOLN HANDICAP (1m)

YR	FORM	WINNER	AGE-WT	RATING	S.P.	DRAW	GOING	TRAINER	JOCKEY	FORM IN YEAR WN-RN	WN DIST.
90	113-120	**EVICHSTAR**	6 7.12	80	33-1	14	FM	J.FitzGerald	A.Munro	1-3	8f
91	1-01111	**AMENABLE**	6 8.01	82	22-1	23	SFT	T.D.Barron	A.Greaves	4-5	8f
92	3012-	**HIGH LOW**	4 8.00	75	16-1	17	GD	W.Haggas	J.Quinn	0-0	
93	102/000-	**HIGH PREMIUM**	5 8.08	80	16-1	5	GD-FM	L.Ramsden	K.Fallon	0-0	
94	003211-	**OUR RITA**	5 8.05	76	16-1	6	GD-FM	Dr.J.Scargill	D.Holland	0-0	
95	200124-	**ROVING MINSTREL**	4 8.03	82	33-1	11	GD-FM	B.McMahon	K.Darley	0-0	
96	000010-	**STONE RIDGE**	4 8.12	87	33-1	6	SFT	R.Hannon	D.O'Neill	0-0	
97	0410-4	**KUALA LIPIS**	4 8.06	86	11-1	21	GD-FM	P.Cole	T.Quinn	0-1	
98	004030-	**HUNTERS OF BRORA**	8 9.00	90	16-1	23	GD	J.Bethell	J.Weaver	0-0	
99	400310-	**RIGHT WING**	5 9.05	100	9-2F	8	GD-SFT	J.Dunlop	T.Quinn	0-0	

AGE (wins-runs): 4-Y-O: 4-115, 5-Y-O: 3-71, **6-Y-O+: 3-53.**
FAVOURITES/SECOND FAVOURITES (strike rate and to a £1 stake): Favs. 10 per cent, -£6.50, S.Favs. 0 per cent, -£12.
AVERAGE WINNING RATING: 84.

Introduction

First run in 1853 and moved to Doncaster in 1965, the Lincoln heralds the start of the Turf Flat season. With fitness at a premium and the draw a major factor, the race has been something of a nightmare for punters, only Cataldi (1985) and Right Wing (1999) justifying favouritism during the past 20 years.

Ten year analysis

Age: Six-year-olds and above have the best strike rate, but age seems largely irrelevant.

Weight/Rating: Dominated by those in the bottom half of the handicap through most of the nineties, the Lincoln has fallen to a pair of relative high-weights during the past two seasons. With that in mind, it would be wrong to continue with the old prejudice against those carrying above 9st.

Draw: While high numbers appeared to have an advantage in the sixties and early seven ties, lower numbers have been preferred recently. That does not preclude a high draw from winning - Kuala Lipis and Hunters Of Brora came from stalls 21 and 23 - but, given a choice, most trainers would plump for a middle to low number.

Eight won during the previous season, seven between seven and ten furlongs and six up until the end of May. Look for a horse that comes to hand early.

While a pipe-opener on the All-Weather can be advantageous - Evichstar, Amenable and Kuala Lipis all ran on the dirt beforehand - it is by no means essential.

Betting: Right Wing broke a 14-year losing run for favourites when winning last season. With second favourites drawing a blank during the past ten seasons, and three successful horses being returned at 33/1, this contest has hardly been punter friendly.

NEWBURY, SATURDAY APRIL 15
LADBROKES SPRING HANDICAP (0-105) (1m)

YR	FORM	WINNER	AGE-WT	RATING	S.P.	DRAW	GOING	TRAINER	JOCKEY	FORM IN YEAR WN-RN	FORM IN YEAR WN DIST.
90	34110-	**WASSL PORT**	4 8.11	88	12-1	2	GD	B.Hills	M.Hills	0-0	
91	30100-2	**ST NINIAN**	5 9.02	91	100-30F	2	GD	M.H.Easterby	L.Piggott	0-1	
92	213314-	**RUDIMENTARY**	4 10.00	103	12-1	2	GD-SFT	H.Cecil	Pat Eddery	0-0	
93	12200-	**TISSISAT**	4 9.01	83	20-1	20	GD	I.Balding	L.Dettori	0-0	
94	01130-3*	**MISSED FLIGHT**	4 9.10	98	6-1(SF)	3	GD-SFT	C.Wall	G.Duffield	0-1	
95	010040-	**STAR MANAGER**	5 8.05	78	20-1	4	GD	P.Cole	T.Quinn	0-0	
96	10/3020-	**ROYAL PHILOSOPHER**	4 8.13	88	25-1	12	GD-SFT	J.Hills	M.Hills	0-0	
**97	02010-2	**HAWKSLEY HILL**	4 9.06	94	5-1F	17	GD-FM	L.Ramsden	J.Fortune	0-1	
98	131030-	**YABINT EL SULTAN**	4 8.12	83	12-1	1	HVY	B.McMahon	R.Cochrane	0-0	
99	20102-1	**BOMB ALASKA**	4 8.00	77	12-1	14	GD-FM	G.B.Balding	J.Egan	1-1	8f

* DISQUALIFIED

** HUNTERS OF BRORA, 7 8.11, 16-1, J.Bethell, D.Holland (8) finished first but was disqualified for interference.

AGE (wins-runners): **4-Y-O: 8-109,** 5-Y-O: 2-51, 6-Y-O+: 0-30.
FAVOURITES/SECOND FAVOURITES (strike rate and to a £1 stake): **Favs. 18 per cent,** -£0.67. S.Favs. 7 per cent, -£7.
AVERAGE WINNING RATING: 88.

Introduction

Usually referred to as the 'Spring Cup', this cracking handicap has produced Group-class winners like Rudimentary, Missed Flight and Hawksley Hill in recent seasons.

Ten Year analysis

Age: Four-year-olds have easily the best record, providing eight of the last ten winners. It is also worth noting that no horse above the age of five has been successful since Star Of A Gunner in 1986. This is not a race for old timers.

Weight/Rating: Eight of the ten winners since 1990 carried at least 8-11.This is probably best left to those in the top half of the handicap.

Draw: A low draw is generally reckoned to be advantageous on the Round Course at Newbury, and six of the last ten did come from single-figure stalls. That said, Bomb Alaska, Hawksley Hill and

Tissisat overcame higher slots, so that is not an insurmountable disadvantage.

Form: Eight won at around a mile in the previous season, but proven fitness seems irrelevant as only four ran earlier in their year. All of those horses ran at Doncaster's Lincoln Meeting, three finishing placed in the Lincoln (one disqualified) and one winning the Spring Mile.
The rule would seem to be that if your selection has run, then make sure he ran well on Town Moor.

Betting: Only two favourites have won since 1990, while no second favourites have been successful. With others going in at 20/1 (twice) and 25/1, shock results are not uncommon.

NEWMARKET, WEDNESDAY APRIL 19
EUROPEAN FREE HANDICAP (LISTED) THREE-YEAR-OLDS (7f)

YR	FORM	WINNER	WT	RATING	S.P.	DRAW	GOING	TRAINER	JOCKEY	FORM IN YEAR WN-RN	WN DIST.
90	01133-	**ANSHAN**	9.07	112	9-2(SF)	6	GD-FM	J.Gosden	Pat Eddery	0-0	
91	213-	**MYSTIKO**	9.02	107	11-1	9	GD-FM	C.Brittain	M.Roberts	0-0	
92	314-	**PURSUIT OF LOVE**	9.01	104	11-4(SF)	1	GD	H.Cecil	Pat Eddery	0-0	
93	122-	**SO FACTUAL**	9.06	112	8-1	7	GD	G.Harwood	Pat Eddery	0-0	
94	13302-3	**BLUEGRASS PRINCE**	8.13	104	10-1	3	GD-SFT	R.Hannon	L.Dettori	0-1	
95	1-	**DIFFIDENT**	9.05	110	11-10F	5	GD-FM	A.Fabre(FR)	M.Kinane	0-0	
96	324212-	**CAYMAN KAI**	9.07	113	7-2JF	4	GD-FM	R.Hannon	Pat Eddery	0-0	
97	013-	**HIDDEN MEADOW**	9.03	108	5-1JF	3	GD	I.Balding	L.Dettori	0-0	
98	1204-	**DESERT PRINCE**	9.05	110	7-1	7	SFT	D.Loder	O.Peslier	0-0	
99	012402-	**BERTOLINI**	9.07	113	5-1	6	GD	J.Gosden	L.Dettori	0-0	

FAVOURITES/SECOND FAVOURITES (strike rate and to a £1 stake): **Favs. 21 per cent, -£1.40,** S.Favs. 15 per cent, -£3.75.
AVERAGE WINNING RATING: 109.

Introduction

The winner of this race usually develops into a high-class performer and will rarely be seen in another handicap. Indeed, Mystiko went on to win the 2000 Guineas, while Anshan and Pursuit Of Love made the frame in the first colts' Classic.

Ten year analysis

Weight/Rating: This is a high-weights race - none of the last 10 carried less than 8-13, six shouldering at least 9-5. As far as ratings are concerned,all ten fit into a band between 104 and 113.

Form: Your selection must have Group race form to his name. Of the last ten only Diffident was unproven at that level, the remaining nine including two who won a Group event in their first season, plus seven who were placed in that sphere. Bluegrass Prince stands alone in that he had a prior outing, and this is best left to seasonal debutantes.

Latest start: It is worth noting that only one last start winner has landed this race since 1990. Eight of the remainder made the frame on their most recent outing.

Betting: Neither favourites nor second favourites can provide a level-stakes profit and the market is not a great guide.

SANDOWN, FRIDAY APRIL 28
SANDOWN MILE (GROUP 2) (1m)

YR	FORM	WINNER	AGE-WT	RATING	S.P.	DRAW	GOING	TRAINER	JOCKEY	FORM IN YEAR WN-RN	W'N DIST.
90	1/41323-	**MARKOFDISTINCTION**	4 9.00	120	9-2	3	GD-FM	L.Cumani	L.Dettori	0-0	
91	141301-	**IN THE GROOVE**	4 9.03	120	15-8(SF)	5	GD-SFT	D.Elsworth	S.Cauthen	0-0	
92	13314-1	**RUDIMENTARY**	4 9.00	117	2-1F	4	GD	H.Cecil	S.Cauthen	1-1	8f
93	404312-	**ALHIJAZ**	4 9.06	120	6-1	3	GD-FM	J.Dunlop	W.Carson	0-0	
94	21211-0	**PENNY DROPS**	5 8.11	99	8-1	6	GD-SFT	Ld Huntingdon	D.Harrison	0-1	
95	30120-3	**MISSED FLIGHT**	5 9.04	117	7-4F	1	GD	C.Wall	G.Duffield	0-1	
96	10210-4	**GABR**	6 9.00	-	13-2	2	GD	R.Armstrong	W.Carson	0-1	
97	2113-2	**WIXIM**	4 9.00	-	5-1(SF)	6	GD-FM	R.Charlton	Pat Eddery	0-1	
98	32100-2	**ALMUSHTARAK**	5 9.00	110	4-1(SF)	6	GD	K.Mahdi	R.Cochrane	0-1	
99	41210-0	**HANDSOME RIDGE**	5 9.00	118	5-1	4	GD-SFT	J.Gosden	L.Dettori	0-1	

AGE (wins-runners): 4-Y-O: 5-57, **5-Y-O: 4-15,** 6-Y-O+: 1-9.

FAVOURITES/SECOND FAVOURITES (strike rate and to a £1 stake): Favs. 20 per cent, -£4.25. **S.Favs. 30 per cent, +£3.87.**

AVERAGE WINNING RATING: 115.

Introduction

Inaugurated in 1985, this race has been won by outstanding horses like Pebbles, Soviet Star, Markofdistinction and In The Groove. While recent winners have not been quite up to that standard, they are all solid Group performers just below the top-class.

Ten year analysis

Age: Five-year-olds have an excellent strike rate, having won four times from just 15 runners since 1989.

Rating: Only Penny Drops (rated 99) went into the race as a seemingly run-of-the-mill performer. As is borne out by our average win rating of 115, this is a race for proven horses.

Form: The last ten scored over seven furlongs or a mile during the preceding season, six in Group company. Seven ran earlier in their year, only one outside Group or Listed company - avoid those stepping-up in class.

Best trial: Newmarket's Earl Of Sefton Stakes is a sound pointer to the result here. The last four ran in that Group Three nine-furlong contest, three making the frame and one finishing unplaced.

Betting: While favourites have a moderate record, second favourites boast a level-stakes profit.

KEMPTON, MONDAY MAY 1
JUBILEE HANDICAP (0-105) (1m)

YR	FORM	WINNER	AGE-WT	RATING	S.P	DRAW	GOING	TRAINER	JOCKEY	FORM IN YEAR WN-RN	WN DIST.
90	004-124	**LANGTRY LADY**	4 8.03	82	14-1	6	FM	M.Ryan	N.Gwilliams	1-3	8f
91	0100-21	**ST NINIAN**	5 9.03	96	9-4F	12	GD	M.H.Easterby	L.Piggott	1-2	8f
92	040012-	**VENUS OBSERVED**	4 9.01	88	14-1	4	GD	H.Candy	A.Armes	0-0	
93	004-430	**PAY HOMAGE**	5 9.01	88	12-1	9	GD	I.Balding	L.Piggott	0-3	
94	11000-0	**CALEMAN**	5 8.12	86	8-1	11	GD-FM	R.Boss	W.Ryan	0-1	
95	12440-0	**DESERT GREEN**	6 9.04	85	7-1	9	GD-FM	R.Hannon	R.Perham	0-1	
96	30020-4	**DESERT GREEN**	7 9.06	95	9-2F	2	GD-FM	R.Hannon	D.O'Neill	0-1	
97	014000-	**AUTUMN COVER**	5 8.03	75	33-1	7	GD	P.Hedger	G.Hind	0-0	
98	00-0330	**TERTIUM**	6 7.11	71	20-1	13	GD	N.Littmoden	R.Mullen	0-4	
99	000-004	**TERTIUM**	7 8.10	86	12-1	10	GD-FM	N.Littmoden	T.Sprake	0-3	

AGE (wins-runners): 4-Y-O: 2-73, 5-Y-O: 4-41, **6-Y-O+: 4-26.**
FAVOURITES/SECOND FAVOURITES (strike rate and to a £1 stake): **Favs. 20 per cent, -£1.25,** S.Favs. 0 per cent, -£12.
AVERAGE WINNING RATING: 85.

Introduction

Like most valuable handicaps run on the metropolitan tracks, this race has lost prestige in recent seasons. That said, it is still very competitive and only won by above-average handicappers.

Ten year analysis

Age: Four of the last five winners were aged six or above and a fair degree of racing experience is obviously helpful.

Weight/Rating: Six of the last ten were rated between 82 and 88, and it would be unwise to support a horse running from a mark much below those figures. Our average winning rating of 85 is an accurate guide to the calibre of horse required.

Draw: While a high draw is marginally preferred, Venus Observed (stall four) and Desert Green (stall two) have conquered a low number in recent seasons.

Form: Nine won from seven to nine furlongs in the previous season. Eight ran earlier in their year, two winning and four making the frame in smart handicap company at seven furlongs or a mile.

Desert Green and Tertium won this race in successive seasons. Kempton is something of a specialist track and those with form here are worth a second glance.

Betting: This is a tough race for the market leaders. Only two favourites and no second favourites have won since 1990.

ASCOT, WEDNESDAY MAY 3
VICTORIA CUP HANDICAP (0-110) (7f)

YR	FORM	WINNER	AGE-WT	RATING	S.P.	DRAW	GOING	TRAINER	JOCKEY	FORM IN YEAR WN-RN	WN DIST.
90	111/000-	**LOMAX**	4 9.03	87	11-1	19	FM	G.Harwood	Pat Eddery	0-0	
91	03310-2	**SKY CLOUD**	5 7.11	76	7-1	3	GD-SFT	R.Akehurst	W.Carson	0-1	
92	240203-	**BAND ON THE RUN**	5 9.00	87	16-1	20	GD-SFT	B.McMahon	T.Quinn	0-0	
93	20000-1	**TENDER MOMENT**	5 7.07	72	16-1	18	GD	C.Brittain	B.Doyle	1-1	7f
94	12004-0	**FACE NORTH**	6 8.01	73	14-1	17	GD-SFT	R.Akehurst	A.Munro	0-1	
95	11300-2	**JAWAAL**	5 8.06	82	7-1F	16	GD-FM	Lady Herries	J.Reid	0-1	
96	032-1	**YEAST**	4 8.09	80	8-1	15	GD-FM	W.Haggas	R.Cochrane	1-1	8f
97	01034-2	**TREGARON**	6 8.13	94	9-1(SF)	11	GD-FM	R.Akehurst	T.Quinn	0-1	
98	ABANDONED - WATERLOGGED										
99	22321-2	**GREAT NEWS**	4 7.12	77	10-1	2	GD	I.Balding	A.Nicholls	0-1	

AGE (wins-runners): 3-Y-O: 0-2, 4-Y-O: 3-83, **5-Y-O: 4-63,** 6-Y-O+: 2-52.
FAVOURITES/SECOND FAVOURITES (strike rate and to a £1 stake): Favs. 7 per cent, -£7. **S.Favs. 8 per cent, -£2.**
AVERAGE WINNING RATING: 81.

Introduction

First run in 1904, this race has maintained a prominent profile and regularly attracts a smart field. Although none of the recent winners made a mark in Group company, the Victoria Cup remains a high-class handicap.

Ten year analysis

Age: Five-year-olds have the best strike rate, but age does not appear particularly significant.

Weight/Rating: Winners have come from all sections of the weights, although only one of the last 10 was rated above 87. If pushed, it could pay to side with something from the bottom half of the handicap.

Draw: Although Great News won from stall two last season, high draws have been advantageous since 1990. Seven of the nine winners since that date came from stalls 11-20.

Form: Six won from six furlongs to a mile in the previous season. More pertinently seven had just one run earlier in their year, two winning and four finishing second. Ensure that your selection has run a promising race this spring.

Betting: Only one favourite and no second favourites have won since 1990. This is a poor race for market leaders.

NEWMARKET, FRIDAY MAY 5
JOCKEY CLUB STAKES (GROUP 2) (1m 4f)

YR	FORM	WINNER	AGE-WT	RATING	S.P.	DRAW	GOING	TRAINER	JOCKEY	FORM IN YEAR WN-RN	WN DIST.
90	332113-	**ROSEATE TERN**	4 8.09	120	17-2	3	GD-FM	L.Cumani	L.Dettori	0-0	
91	011/21-1	**ROCK HOPPER**	4 8.07	111	8-11F	6	GD	Sir M.Stoute	Pat Eddery	1-1	12f
92	0/00000-	**SAPIENCE**	6 8.12	-	40-1	6	GD	D.Elsworth	R.Cochrane	0-0	
93	1/13-	**ZINAAD**	4 8.09	107	3-1F	3	GD	Sir M.Stoute	W.Swinburn	0-0	
94	0/4000-2	**SILVER WISP**	5 8.09	101	20-1	4	GD-FM	D.Nicholson	M.Hills	0-1	
95	4/00100-	**ONLY ROYALE**	6 8.11	119	4-1	5	GD	L.Cumani	L.Dettori	0-0	
96	120112-	**RIYADIAN**	4 8.09	120	10-11F	2	GD-FM	P.Cole	T.Quinn	0-0	
97	122221-	**TIME ALLOWED**	4 8.06	109	13-2	3	GD	Sir M.Stoute	J.Reid	0-0	
98	333123-	**ROMANOV**	4 8.09	115	5-1	5	GD-SFT	P.Chapple-Hyam	J.Reid	0-0	
99	140221-	**SILVER PATRIARCH**	5 9.00	123	9-2JF	7	GD	J.Dunlop	Pat Eddery	0-0	

AGE (wins-runners): 4-Y-O: 6-61, 5-Y-O: 2-14, 6-Y-O+: 2-12.
FAVOURITES/SECOND FAVOURITES (strike rate and to a £1 stake): **Favs. 36 per cent, +£2.14,** S.Favs. 0 per cent, -£11.
AVERAGE WINNING RATING: 114.
TOP TRAINER (wins-runners, strike rate and to a £1 stake): **Sir Michael Stoute (3-10, 30 per cent, +£3.23).**

Introduction

While this race always attracts a smart field, the successful horse is seldom worth following. Of the ten winners since 1990, Roseate Tern, Sapience, Zinaad, Silver Wisp, Only Royale, Riyadian, Time Allowed and Romanov all failed to score during the remainder of the campaign.

Ten year analysis

Age: Four-year-olds are the most prolific age group, although their older rivals have superior strike rates.

Weight/Rating: As is borne out by our average win rating (114), this is often won by a proven horse just short of the very top-class.

Form: Seasonal debutantes are strongly favoured - eight have won since 1990. Seven won a middle-distance Group race during the previous season, underlining the fact that this is best left to established horses.

Betting: Four winning favourites in ten seasons is a fair return and this is a decent race for market leaders. Unfortunately second favourites drew a blank during the same period.

Top Trainer: There is no better trainer of older horses than Sir Michael Stoute. That being so, it is no surprise to find that he has sent out three winners from ten runners since 1990.

NEWMARKET, SATURDAY MAY 6
2000 GUINEAS STAKES (GROUP 1) THREE-YEAR-OLD COLTS AND FILLIES (1m)

YR	FORM	WINNER	WT	RATING	S.P.	DRAW	GOING	TRAINER	JOCKEY	FORM IN YEAR WN-RN	WN DIST.
90	3211-1	**TIROL**	9.00	110	9-1	1	GD-FM	R.Hannon	M.Kinane	1-1	8f
91	213-1	**MYSTIKO**	9.00	107	13-2(SF)	5	GD	C.Brittain	M.Roberts	1-1	7f
92	11111-4	**RODRIGO DE TRIANO**	9.00	122	6-1	3	GD	P.Chapple-Hyam	L.Piggott	0-1	
93	1111-2	**ZAFONIC**	9.00	125	5-6F	10	GD	A.Fabre(FR)	Pat Eddery	0-1	
94	13101-	**MISTER BAILEYS**	9.00	115	16-1	21	GD-FM	M.Johnston	J.Weaver	0-0	
95	1111-1	**PENNEKAMP**	9.00	124	9-2(SF)	11	GD-FM	A.Fabre(FR)	T.Jarnet	1-1	7f
96	21-	**MARK OF ESTEEM**	9.00	108	8-1	2	GD-FM	S.Bin Suroor	L.Dettori	0-1	
97	411-	**ENTREPRENEUR**	9.00	103	11-2(SF)	4	GD	M.Stoute	M.Kinane	0-0	

98	11211-	**KING OF KINGS**	9.00	111	7-2(SF)	17	GD-SFT	A.O'Brien(IR)	M.Kinane	0-0
99	11-	**ISLAND SANDS**	9.00	-	10-1	3	GD-FM	S.Bin Suroor	L.Dettori	0-0

FAVOURITES/SECOND FAVOURITES (strike rate and to a £1 stake): Favs. 10 per cent, -£8.17, **S.Favs. 40 per cent, +£14.**
AVERAGE WINNING RATING: 114.

Introduction

While the profile of the 2000 Guineas has dipped slightly - none of the last ten winners were 'great' horses - it remains a tremendous event. One can only hope that it is not too long before another Brigadier Gerard, Nijinsky, Dancing Brave or Nashwan grabs first prize.

Ten year analysis

Weight/Rating: Only Rodrigo de Triano (rated 122), Zafonic (125) and Pennekamp (124) were top-class juveniles. Do not be afraid to look lower down the Free Handicap when looking for a potential 2000 Guineas winner.

Form: The last ten won as two-year-olds, although only six managed to land a Group race. Success at that level as a juvenile is not essential.
While traditionalists may disagree, a prep race is no longer necessary - the last four winners were all making their seasonal reappearance. Note that two of this quartet were from the Godolphin camp and had come through strenuous trials in Dubai. Sheikh Mohammed's team do not send half-baked horses to contest a Classic.

Latest start: Eight won their latest start and it would seem best to avoid colts coming here on the back of a defeat.

Betting: Only the odds-on Zafonic has justified favouritism since 1990. However, second favourites have a useful 40 per cent strike rate and healthy level-stakes profit.

Top trainers: While there are no outstanding training trends, it is interesting to note that Saeed Bin Suroor (Godolphin) and Andre Fabre have both won the race twice in the past seven seasons.

NEWMARKET, SUNDAY MAY 7
1000 GUINEAS STAKES (GROUP 1) THREE-YEAR-OLD FILLIES (1m)

YR	FORM	WINNER	WT	RATING	S.P.	DRAW	GOING	TRAINER	JOCKEY	FORM IN YEAR WN-RN	WN DIST.
90	121-1	**SALSABIL**	9.00	114	6-4F	5	GD-FM	J.Dunlop	W.Carson	1-1	7f
91	111-1	**SHADAYID**	9.00	120	4-6F	13	GD	J.Dunlop	W.Carson	1-1	7f
92	122-2	**HATOOF**	9.00	114	5-1(SF)	12	GD	C.Head(FR)	W.Swinburn	0-1	
93	2111-3	**SAYYEDATI**	9.00	115	4-1(SF)	4	GD	C.Brittain	W.Swinburn	0-1	
94	12-	**LAS MENINAS**	9.00	114	12-1	1	GD	T.Stack(IR)	J.Reid	0-0	
95	1213-2	**HARAYIR**	9.00	118	5-1(SF)	2	GD-FM	W.Hern	R.Hills	0-1	
96	11-1	**BOSRA SHAM**	9.00	118	10-11F	11	GD-FM	H.Cecil	Pat Eddery	1-1	7f
97	13-4	**SLEEPYTIME**	9.00	111	5-1	3	GD	H.Cecil	K.Fallon	0-1	
98	1214-	**CAPE VERDI**	9.00	109	100-30F	7	GD	S.bin Suroor	L. Dettori	0-0	
99	12100-1	**WINCE**	9.00	106	4-1F	19	GD-FM	H.Cecil	K.Fallon	1-1	7f

FAVOURITES/SECOND FAVOURITES (strike rate and to a £1 stake): Favs. 45 per cent, +£4.40, **S.Favs. 23 per cent, +£4.**

AVERAGE WINNING RATING: 114.

TOP TRAINER (wins-runs, strike rate and to a £1 stake): **Henry Cecil (3-9, 33 per cent, +£3.91).**

Introduction

First run in 1814, the 1000 Guineas has been won by some wonderful fillies over the past two decades, Pebbles, Oh So Sharp, Midway Lady, Miesque, Salsabil, Hatoof and Bosra Sham all figuring on the roll of honour.

However, it is ten years since any horse completed the Guineas-Oaks double, hinting that this has become a race for specialist milers.

Ten year analysis

Weight/Rating: Nine of the last ten earned a mark on the European Free Handicap at the end of their two-year-old campaign (the exception is Wince), so your selection should have shown high class form as a juvenile. Our average winning rating of 114 is a fair indicator of the level required to win here.

Form: All ten won as juveniles, seven over seven furlongs or a mile and six in Group races.

A prep race is a definite help - only two seasonal debutantes have scored since 1990 - four winning and four making the frame in a seven furlong Group/Listed contest beforehand.

Latest start: Four won and six were placed on their latest start. Any who were unplaced last time can be ignored.

Best trial: Newbury's Fred Darling Stakes (now run as the Dubai Duty Free Stakes) is easily the best trial. No fewer than five of the last ten used that contest as their Guineas prep, four winning and one finishing fourth.

It is interesting to note that the five who ran in the Fred Darling were trained by either John Dunlop or Henry Cecil.

Betting: This is a race where the market speaks truthfully. Favourites have won five of the last ten runnings, while second favourites have scored on three occasions.

Since 1990, only Las Meninas (12/1) has started at longer than 5/1 and this is not an outsiders' race.

Trainers: Henry Cecil has saddled three winners from nine runners since 1990, all his successes coming in the past four seasons. Any Warren Place runner must be treated with the utmost respect.

CHESTER, WEDNESDAY MAY 10
CHESTER CUP HANDICAP (2m 2f 147y)

YR	FORM	WINNER	AGE-WT	RATING	S.P	DRAW	GOING	TRAINER	JOCKEY	FORM IN YEAR WN-RN	WN DIST.
90	0113-02	**TRAVELLING LIGHT**	4 9.01	81	5-2F	10	GD	L.Ramsden	A.Munro	0-2	
91	2/211	**STAR PLAYER**	5 8.10	79	9-2(SF)	6	GD	J.Baker	L.Dettori	2-3	16f
92	3002-24	**WELSHMAN**	6 7.08	58	11-1	6	GD	M.Blanshard	J.Quinn	0-2	
93	3124/0/-1	**RODEO STAR**	7 7.13	65	9-1	16	GD-FM	N.Tinkler	N.Carlisle	1-1	16f
94	33000-3	**DOYCE**	5 7.10	65	14-1	5	GD-FM	R.Williams	G.Bardwell	0-1	
95	0040-00	**TOP CEES**	5 8.08	72	8-1	15	GD-FM	L.Ramsden	K.Fallon	0-2	
96	000111-	**MERIT**	4 7.10	74	11-2	12	GD	P.Cole	J.Quinn	0-0	
97	3/0100-2	**TOP CEES**	7 8.11	87	11-2	6	SFT	L.Ramsden	J.Fortune	0-1	
98	101/33/2-	**SILENCE IN COURT**	7 9.00	88	13-2	9	GD	A.Bailey	A.Mackay	0-0	
99	20024-1	**RAINBOW HIGH**	4 9.00	103	4-1F	13	GD-FM	B.Hills	M.Hills	1-1	16f

AGE (wins-runners): 4-Y-O: 3-57, **5-Y-O: 3-42,** 6-Y-O+: 4-66.
FAVOURITES/SECOND FAVOURITES (strike rate and to a £1 stake): **Favs. 18 per cent, -£2.50,** S.Favs. 8 per cent, -£6.50.
AVERAGE WINNING RATING: 77.

Introduction

Inaugurated in 1824, the Chester Cup went through a fallow period in the early nineties, but attracted a top-class field last year, when Group One winner Invermark headed the weights ahead of crack stayers like Rainbow High and Generosity. Hopefully this revival was not a flash in the pan.

Ten year analysis

Age: There is little to choose between the various age groups, five-year-olds having marginally the better strike rate.

Weight/Rating: Rainbow High (rated 103) became the first 'class' winner of this race for some time when he scored last year. Him apart, no recent winner was rated above 88.

Form: Winning form last season is unimportant - only five scored - and it is more useful to note that three won and four made the frame in a handicap over at least a mile and three-quarters beforehand.

Latest start: As four won and five were placed on their latest start, this is not a race for those who disappointed last time.

Best trial: Two of the last three ran in the two mile handicap at Newbury's Greenham Meeting in mid-April. Known as the Levy Board Handicap in recent seasons, this race could develop into a leading Chester Cup trial.

Betting: This is not a great race for favourite backers. However, only one real outsider (Doyce) has won since 1990, and it should pay to side with relatively fancied horses when making your selection.

YORK, WEDNESDAY MAY 17
DANTE STAKES (GROUP 2) THREE-YEAR-OLDS (1m 2f 85y)

YR	FORM	WINNER	WT	RATING	S.P.	DRAW	GOING	TRAINER	JOCKEY	FORM IN YEAR WN-RN	WN DIST.
90	2-12	**SANGLAMORE**	9.00	-	11-2(SF)	5	GD	R.Charlton	Pat Eddery	1-2	10f
91	01-30	**ENVIRONMENT FRIEND**	9.00	-	20-1	4	GD-FM	J.Fanshawe	G.Duffield	0-2	
92	213-10	**ALNASR ALWASHEEK**	9.00	109	7-2(SF)	2	GD-FM	M.Stoute	S.Cauthen	1-2	8f
93	111-1	**TENBY**	9.00	122	1-3F	1	GD	H.Cecil	Pat Eddery	1-1	10f
94	01123-2	**ERHAAB**	9.00	108	11-2	1	FM	J.Dunlop	W.Carson	0-1	
95	12-	**CLASSIC CLICHE**	8.11	108	9-1	8	GD	S.Bin Suroor	W.Swinburn	0-0	
96	1221-2	**GLORY OF DANCER**	8.11	111	3-1(SF)	2	GD-FM	P.Kelleway	O.Peslier	0-1	
97	21113-2	**BENNY THE DIP**	8.11	113	100-30F	4	GD	J.Gosden	O.Peslier	0-1	
98	121311-	**SARATOGA SPRINGS**	8.11	116	4-1	6	GD	A.O'Brien(IR)	M.Kinane	0-0	
99	20-1	**SALFORD EXPRESS**	8.11	102	12-1	2	SFT	D.Elsworth	T.Quinn	1-1	11f

FAVOURITES/SECOND FAVOURITES (strike rate and to a £1 stake): Favs. 17 per cent, -£6.34. **S.Favs. 30 per cent, +£5.**
AVERAGE WINNING RATING: 111.

Introduction

Our most valuable Derby trial, the Dante Stakes has produced Epsom heroes like Shirley Heights, Shahrastani, Reference Point, Erhaab and Benny the Dip.

Ten year analysis

Weight/Rating: While it has been won by some cracking horses, the average win rating is a relatively low 111. That indicates that this generally falls to progressive horses.

Form: Eight won as two-year-olds, all over at least seven furlongs. Eight ran once or twice earlier in their year (six in Group or Listed races) four winning and only two finishing unplaced. Note that only one had run in the 2000 Guineas. This is not a race for any who failed in the mile Classic.

Latest start: Only two were unplaced on their latest start. Avoid those attempting to retrieve a ost reputation.

Betting: Favourites have a poor record, while second favourites boast a healthy level-stakes profit. Do not be afraid to look beyond the market leader.

YORK, THURSDAY MAY 18
YORKSHIRE CUP (GROUP 2) (1m 6f)

YR	FORM	WINNER	AGE-WT	RATING	S.P.	DRAW	GOING	TRAINER	JOCKEY	FORM IN YEAR WN-RN	WN DIST.
90	21110-1	**BRAASHEE**	4 8.09	-	11-8F	3	GD	A.Stewart	M.Roberts	1-1	13f
91	112101-	**ARZANNI**	4 8.09	-	5-1	6	GD-FM	L.Cumani	L.Dettori	0-0	
92	21320-0	**ROCK HOPPER**	5 8.13	122	100-30F	1	GD-FM	Sir M.Stoute	Pat Eddery	0-1	
93	3031-42	**ASSESSOR**	4 9.00	115	9-1	5	GD	R.Hannon	T.Quinn	0-2	
94	1423-40	**KEY TO MY HEART**	4 8.09	102	16-1	6	FM	D.Moffatt	J.Reid	0-2	
95	200311-	**MOONAX**	4 8.09	116	11-4F	1	GD	B.Hills	Pat Eddery	0-0	
96	2/14201-	**CLASSIC CLICHE**	4 9.00	119	2-1(SF)	5	GD-FM	S.Bin Suroor	M.Kinane	0-0	
97	11121-4	**CELERIC**	5 8.09	111	7-2(SF)	2	GD	D.Morley	Pat Eddery	0-1	
98	11032-2	**BUSY FLIGHT**	5 8.09	116	2-1F	6	GD	B.Hills	M.Hills	0-1	
99	10110-3	**CHURLISH CHARM**	4 8.09	102	25-1	1	SFT	R.Hannon	R.Hughes	0-1	

AGE (wins-runners): 4-Y-O: 7-39, 5-Y-O: 3-13, 6-Y-O+: 0-18.
FAVOURITES/SECOND FAVOURITES (strike rate and to a £1 stake): **Favs. 33 per cent**, +£1.45, S.Favs. 18 per cent, -£3.50.
AVERAGE WINNING RATING: 113.

Introduction

Every St Leger winner during the nineties was kept in training as a four-year-old. As Moonax and Classic Cliche have proved recently, this race is an excellent early-season target for horses of that type.

Ten year analysis

Age: Four-year-olds have the best record numerically, although five-year-olds have a better strike rate. Stick to horses from these age groups.

Weight/Rating: Three horses - Assessor, Moonax and Classic Cliché - have defied the Group One penalty. Class can overcome extra poundage in this contest.

Form: Nine won at least twice during the previous season, seven landing a Group or Listed contest. Generally, this is a race for established horses. Seven had one or two starts earlier in their year, only one running outside Group or Listed events. This is more important than a recent victory (only Braashee managed to score during his preparation).

Latest Start: Eight ran in a Group race on their latest start, none below a mile and a half. Avoid any taking a big step-up in trip.

Betting: This is a fair race for favourites, four having won since 1990. Still, Key To My Heart (16/1) and Churlish Charm (25/1) prove that shocks can occur.

NEWBURY, SATURDAY MAY 20
LOCKINGE STAKES (GROUP 1) (1m)

										FORM IN YEAR	
YR	FORM	WINNER	AGE-WT	RATING	S.P.	DRAW	GOING	TRAINER	JOCKEY	WN-RN	WN DIST.
90	0111-01	SAFAWAN	4 9.00	106	5-1	4	GD-FM	Sir M.Stoute	W.Swinburn	1-2	7f
91	14322-1	POLAR FALCON	4 9.00	110	3-1(SF)	2	GD	J.Hammond(FR)	L.Piggott	1-1	8f
92	233411-	SELKIRK	4 9.05	128	5-2(SF)	5	GD	I.Balding	R.Cochrane	0-0	
93	0331-01	SWING LOW	4 9.00	110	12-1	6	GD	R.Hannon	L.Piggott	1-2	7f
94	02320-4	EMPEROR JONES	4 9.00	114	11-2	9	GD	J.Gosden	L.Dettori	0-1	
95	411121-	SOVIET LINE	5 9.00	117	2-1F	4	GD-FM	Sir M.Stoute	W.Swinburn	0-0	
96	0320-02	SOVIET LINE	6 9.00	120	13-2	1	SFT	Sir M.Stoute	T.Quinn	0-2	
97	12301-2	FIRST ISLAND	5 9.00	123	11-4(SF)	1	GD-SFT	G.Wragg	M.Hills	0-1	

98	2121*-20	CAPE CROSS	4 9.00	118	20-1	8	GD-FM	S. Bin Suroor	D.O'Donohoe	0-2
99	232110-	FLY TO THE STARS	5 9.00	118	9-1	6	SFT	S.Bin Suroor	W.Supple	0-0

*Disqualified.

AGE (wins-runners): 4-Y-O: 6-52, 5-Y-O: 3-19, 6-Y-O+: 1-5.
FAVOURITES/SECOND FAVOURITES (strike rate and to a £1 stake): Favs. 10 per cent, -£7, **S.Favs. 25 per cent, -£0.25.**
AVERAGE WINNING RATING: 118..
TOP TRAINER (wins-runners, strike rate and to a £1 stake): **Sir Michael Stoute (3-6, 50 per cent, +£10.50).**

Introduction

Granted Group One status in 1995, this is an enticing early-season target for Europe's finest milers. The Godolphin team seem particularly keen on the race, and have won the last two runnings with the lesser-fancied of two entrants. Everything they run here must be treated with respect.

Ten year analysis

Age: Four-year-olds have weighed in with six winners, but five-year-olds boast a superior strike rate.

Weight/Rating: No horse rated below 117 has won this race since it was upgraded to Group One in 1995. Avoid those who have yet to prove themselves against top-class opposition.

Form: All ten won in the previous season, nine over a mile, seven in Group company. Seven ran earlier in their year (only one outside Group or Listed events), just three winning. A recent strike is not essential.

Best trial: The Group Two Sandown Mile (run at Sandown on April 28) has been a useful guide. Four Lockinge winners ran in that contest, three making the frame and one finishing unplaced.

Betting: A poor race for market leaders. Only one favourite has won since 1990, while second favourites also yield a level-stakes loss.

Top trainers: Sir Michael Stoute is a wonderful trainer of older horses and heads the list here, saddling three winners from six runners since 1990. Saeed Bin Suroor is also a force to reckon with. Fly To The Stars and Cape Cross have won the last two runnings for Godolphin's handler, both beating better-fancied stablemates.

HAYDOCK, SATURDAY MAY 27
TOTE CREDIT SILVER BOWL HANDICAP (0-110) THREE-YEAR-OLDS (1m)

YR	FORM	WINNER	WT	RATING	S.P.	DRAW	GOING	TRAINER	JOCKEY	FORM IN YEAR WN-RN	WN DIST.
90	2143-01	**CASHTAL DAZZLER**	7.07	83	14-1	7	GD-FM	J.Berry	L.Charnock	1-2	8f
91	001-214	**TAKADDUM**	9.03	93	5-1(SF)	2	GD-FM	P.Walwyn	G.Baxter	1-3	7f
92	311-3	**SHARPITOR**	9.00	92	13-2	4	GD-FM	W.Jarvis	J.Reid	0-1	
93	104-34	**MOORISH**	8.02	80	11-1	8	SFT	P.Cole	T.McLaughlin	0-2	
94	01-40	**DANCE TURN**	9.00	90	25-1	1	GD-FM	R.Armstrong	R.Price	0-2	
95	220-013	**SONIC BOY**	9.07	104	9-1	7	GD-SFT	R.F.J.Houghton	J.Quinn	1-3	8f
96	032-2	**WINTER ROMANCE**	9.00	90	9-4F	8	GD-SFT	E.Dunlop	Paul Eddery	0-1	
97	2-21	**ALEZAL**	9.01	90	5-2F	6	GD-SFT	W.Jarvis	S.Sanders	1-2	8f
98	022-1	**FRENCH CONNECTION**	7.09	77	12-1	7	GD-SFT	J.Berry	P.Fessey	1-1	9f
99	3-12	**DATE**	8.13	97	12-1	16	GD	E.Dunlop	W.Ryan	1-2	7f

FAVOURITES/SECOND FAVOURITES (strike rate and to a £1 stake): Favs. 17 per cent, -£5.25, **S.Favs. 9 per cent,** -£5.
AVERAGE WINNING RATING: 90.

Introduction

Class horses like Silver Season, Spanish Pool, Safawan, Sharpitor, Dance Turn, Winter Romance and Alezal have won this valuable handicap. Do not be surprised if their successor makes a mark in Listed or Group company.

Ten year analysis

Weight/Rating: Seven were rated 90 or above – this is a race for above average horses.

Form: Only one maiden has won, although it does not seem to matter if your selection scored as a two or three-year-old. More interesting is that only one had more than six career starts under his belt, while none of the last three had run in a handicap. That burgeoning trend could be worth following.

Latest Start: Three won and six were placed on their latest start. This is not a race for horses coming back from a poor effort.

Betting: With winners returning at 11/1, 12/1 (twice), 14/1 and 25/1, it should pay to look beyond the market leaders.

Top trainers: There are no outstanding training trends, although William Jarvis and Ed Dunlop have managed to get on the score sheet twice. Keep on the right side of their entrants.

CURRAGH, SATURDAY MAY 27
IRISH 2000 GUINEAS (GROUP 1) THREE-YEAR-OLD COLTS AND FILLIES (1m)

YR	FORM	WINNER	WT	S.P.	GOING	TRAINER	JOCKEY	FORM IN YEAR WN-RN	WN DIST.
90	3211-11	**TIROL**	9.00	5-4F	GD	R.Hannon	Pat Eddery	2-2	8f
91	2110-21	**FOURSTARS ALLSTAR**	9.00	9-1	GD	L.O'Brien(USA)	M.Smith	1-2	8f
92	1111-41	**RODRIGO DE TRIANO**	9.00	8-11F	GD-SFT	P.Chapple-Hyam	L.Piggott	1-2	8f
93	11-42	**BARATHEA**	9.00	4-7F	SFT	L.Cumani	M.Roberts	0-2	
94	3114-12	**TURTLE ISLAND**	9.00	5-4F	HVY	P.Chapple-Hyam	J.Reid	1-2	7f
95	1-1	**SPECTRUM**	9.00	10-3(SF)	GD-FM	P.Chapple-Hyam	J.Reid	1-1	8f
96	11-32	**SPINNING WORLD**	9.00	7-4F	GD-SFT	J.Pease(FR)	C.Asmussen	0-2	
97	2110-21	**DESERT KING**	9.00	3-1(SF)	GD-SFT	A.O'Brien(IR)	C.Roche	1-2	7f
98	1204-13	**DESERT PRINCE**	9.00	8-1	GD-FM	D.Loder	O.Peslier	1-2	7f
99	2-11	**SAFFRON WALDON**	9.00	12-1	GD	A.O'Brien(IR)	O.Peslier		

FAVOURITES/SECOND FAVOURITES (strike rate and to a £1 stake): **Favs. 50 per cent, +£0.55**, S.Favs. 20 per cent, -£1.67.
TOP TRAINER (wins-runners, strike rate and to a £1 stake): **Peter Chapple-Hyam (3-7, 43 per cent, +£1.31).**

Introduction

Despite being 112 years younger than its English counterpart, this race is no poor relation to the Newmarket Classic. Recent winners like Rodrigo de Triano, Barathea, Spinning World and Desert Prince were outstanding performers.

Ten year analysis

Form: Nine won as two-year-olds, seven over seven furlongs or a mile. Nine had two starts earlier in their year, eight winning and none finishing out of the frame.

Latest start: Six ran in 'a Guineas' on their latest start, two winning, three finishing second and one third.

Best trial: There are no outstanding trials, although both the English and French 2000 Guineas have produced three Irish 2000 Guineas heroes since 1990. A good run in either of those contests is a fair recommendation.

Betting: Favourites boast a 50 per cent strike rate, although only one has scored in the past five seasons. The tide has taken a turn for the worse as far as market leaders are concerned.

Top trainers: Only Aidan O'Brien has managed to keep this prize at home in the past decade. Without him, the English and French raiders would have run amok.

CURRAGH, SUNDAY MAY 28
IRISH 1000 GUINEAS (GROUP 1) THREE-YEAR-OLD FILLIES (1m)

								FORM IN YEAR	
YR	FORM	WINNER	WT	S.P.	GOING	TRAINER	JOCKEY	WN-RN	WN DIST.
90	213-201	**IN THE GROOVE**	9.00	5-1(SF)	GD	D.Elsworth	S.Cauthen	1-3	10f
91	1121-12	**KOOYONGA**	9.00	4-1(SF)	GD	M.Kauntze(IR)	W.O'Connor	1-2	7f
92	1111-2	**MARLING**	9.00	4-5F	GD	G.Wragg	W.Swinburn	0-1	
93	02014-1	**NICER**	9.00	8-1	GD-SFT	B.Hills	M.Hills	1-1	8f
94	4133-14	**MEHTHAAF**	9.00	5-2(SF)	GD-SFT	J.Dunlop	W.Carson	1-2	7f
95	31-1	**RIDGEWOOD PEARL**	9.00	9-4(SF)	GD	J.Oxx(IR)	C.Roche	1-1	7f
96	1323-2	**MATIYA**	9.00	5-1	GD-SFT	B.Hanbury	W.Carson	0-1	
97	04200-1	**CLASSIC PARK**	9.00	20-1	GD-SFT	A.O'Brien(IR)	S.Craine	1-1	7f
98	3101-0	**TARASCON**	9.00	12-1	GD-FM	T.Stack(IR)	J.Spencer	0-1	
99	31031-0	**HULA ANGEL**	9.00	16-1	GD	B.Hills		M.Hills	0-1

FAVOURITES/SECOND FAVOURITES (strike rate and to a £1 stake): Favs. 20 per cent, -£5.58, **S.Favs. 33 per cent, +£5.75.**

Introduction

This is one of Europe's weaker Classics. Fillies like Nicer, Matiya, Classic Park, Tarascon and Hula Angel were not among the leaders of their generation.

Ten year analysis

Form: All ten scored as juveniles, five winning and three making the frame in Group company. Each of the winners ran earlier in her year (seven just once), six landing a Group or Listed event. This hoists the total of previous Group winners to seven and your selection should have scored in that grade.

Latest start: None ran outside Group or Listed company on their latest start. Avoid those stepping out of maiden or minor events.

Best trial: Seven ran in the 1000 Guineas at Newmarket, four making the frame and three finishing unplaced. Note, however, that no filly has managed to complete the English-Irish 1000 Guineas double, Harayir, Las Meninas and Wince being recent expensive failures.

Betting: We have to go back to Marling (1992) to find a winning favourite. The last three scorers returned at double figure prices and outsiders have every chance.

Top trainers: The home team have a fair record, scoring four times since 1990, including three of the past five renewals. Barry Hills' two wins are also noteworthy; his raiders must be treated with respect.

SANDOWN, MONDAY MAY 29
TEMPLE STAKES (GROUP 2) (5f)

YR	FORM	WINNER	AGE-WT	RATING	S.P.	DRAW	GOING	TRAINER	JOCKEY	FORM IN YEAR WN-RN	WN DIST.
90	12-012	**DAYJUR**	3 8.08	105	11-2	4	GD-FM	W.Hern	W.Carson	1-3	6f
91	1110-21	**ELBIO**	4 9.03	-	11-8F	6	GD	P.Makin	W.Swinburn	1-2	5f
92	1401-40	**SNAADEE**	5 9.03	107	14-1	6	GD-FM	Sir M.Stoute	Pat Eddery	0-2	
93	00000-1	**PARIS HOUSE**	4 9.07	113	9-1(SF)	7	GD-FM	J.Berry	J.Carroll	1-1	5f
94	11131-1	**LOCHSONG**	6 9.07	123	4-9F	9	GD-SFT	I.Balding	L.Dettori	1-1	5f
95	0020-11	**MIND GAMES**	3 8.08	117	10-11F	5	GD-FM	J.Berry	J.Carroll	2-2	5f
96	113000-	**MIND GAMES**	4 9.07	117	7-2F	9	GD-SFT	J.Berry	J.Carroll	0-0	
97	103120-	**CROFT POOL**	6 9.03	107	20-1	9	GD-FM	J.Glover	G.Carter	0-0	
98	0000-01	**BOLSHOI**	6 9.03	108	10-1	2	GD	J.Berry	C.Lowther	1-2	5f
99	4110-32	**TIPSY CREEK**	5 9.03	111	7-1	5	GD	B.Hanbury	R.Hills	0-2	

AGE (wins-runners): 3-Y-O: 2-21, 4-Y-O: 3-31, 5-Y-O: 2-16, **6-Y-O+: 3-12.**
FAVOURITES/SECOND FAVOURITES (strike rate and to a £1 stake): **Favs. 40 per cent, +£0.22,** S.Favs. 8 per cent, -£7.50.
AVERAGE WINNING RATING: 112.

Introduction

Besides being a cracking race in its own right, this is an excellent trial for Royal Ascot's King's Stand Stakes. Dayjur, Elbio, Lochsong and Bolshoi have all completed that big-race double since 1990.

Ten year analysis

Age: There is no strong age bias, although six-year-olds and above have the best strike rate.

Weight/Rating: Only Lochsong (123) had a truly top-class rating when scoring here. Most of the other winners appeared to fall just below the top-class, although several went on to prove themselves in the highest grade.

Form: All ten won in the previous season, seven demonstrating their class by landing a Group or Listed contest. Eight ran beforehand (Mind Games and Croft Pool have proved that seasonal debutantes can score), six winning a five or six-furlong non-handicap.

Latest start: Of the eight who ran earlier in their year, only the inconsistent Snaadee finished unplaced on his latest start.

Best trial: Newmarket's Palace House Stakes (run on 2000 Guineas Day) is an excellent pointer to the result. Five of the last ten ran in that event, four winning and one finishing unplaced.

Betting: Favourites boast a useful 40 per cent strike rate, but that only translates to a modest level-stakes profit.

SANDOWN, MONDAY MAY 29
DOUBLEPRINT RATED STAKES (0-105) (1m)

YR	FORM	WINNER	AGE-WT	RATING	S.P.	DRAW	GOING	TRAINER	JOCKEY	FORM IN YEAR WN-RN	WN DIST.
90	3/2210-3	**TAFILA**	4 8.07	89	7-1	6	GD-FM	W.Jarvis	W.Carson	0-1	
91	-12	**FANMORE**	3 9.07	105	9-2JF	3	GD	G.Harwood	Pat Eddery	1-2	8f
92	4210-04	**PAY HOMAGE**	4 9.04	91	7-1	9	GD-FM	I.Balding	M.Hills	0-2	
93	4-43011	**PAY HOMAGE**	5 9.05	98	8-1	7	GD-FM	I.Balding	M.Hills	2-5	8f
94	1/03110-	**DAWNING STREET**	6 9.07	105	15-2	9	GD-SFT	J.Dunlop	Pat Eddery	0-0	
95	4011-00	**DANCE TURN**	4 9.03	99	10-3(SF)	4	GD-FM	R.Armstrong	M.Hills	0-2	
96	1202-00	**BLOMBERG**	4 9.01	93	20-1	8	GD-SFT	J.Fanshawe	J.Carroll	0-2	
97	01/32-3	**INSATIABLE**	4 9.04	96	5-2F	7	GD-FM	Sir M.Stoute	M.Kinane	0-1	
98	0022-33	**FOR YOUR EYES ONLY**	4 9.00	90	15-2	9	GD	T.D.Easterby	J.Weaver	0-2	
99	110420-	**LONESOME DUDE**	4 9.04	96	11-2JF	9	GD	Sir M.Stoute	G.Mosse	0-0	

AGE (wins-runners): 3-Y-O: 1-15, 4-Y-O: 7-59, **5-Y-O: 1-23,** 6-Y-O+: 1-21.

FAVOURITES/SECOND FAVOURITES (strike rate and to a £1 stake): **Favs. 20 per cent, +£0.50,** S.Favs. 7 per cent, -£10.67.

AVERAGE WINNING RATING: 96.

Introduction

Formerly run as the Whitsun Cup, this is traditionally a sound trial for the Royal Hunt Cup. Keep the principals in mind for that popular cavalry charge at Royal Ascot.

Ten year analysis

Age: While four-year-olds have had more than double the runners of any other age group, they remain the dominant force. Seven wins in ten runnings is a fair record by any standards.

Weight/Rating: Only one of the last ten carried less than 9st. This is a top-class limited handicap and those towards the head of the weights are preferred.

Form: Seven won during the previous season, although it is more interesting to note that only two scored earlier in their year. Overexposed horses will struggle in a race as competitive as this, as is borne out by the fact that only Pay Homage ran more than twice during his preparation.

Latest start: Only one last-start scorer has won since 1990. Stick with those who have hinted that they are approaching a peak.

Betting: Favourites have a respectable record, while second favourites show a heavy level-stakes loss. The market is not a particularly reliable guide.

Top trainer: No outstanding trends, although it is interesting to see that Sir Michael Stoute has landed two of the last three renewals.

NEWMARKET, SATURDAY JUNE 3
CORAL SPRINT HANDICAP (0-105) THREE-YEAR-OLDS (6f)

YR	FORM	WINNER	WT	RATING	S.P.	DRAW	GOING	TRAINER	JOCKEY	FORM IN YEAR RN-WN	WN DIST.
90	20-1112	**CASE LAW**	9.07	99	9-1	11	GD-FM	Sir M.Prescott	G.Duffield	3-4	6f
91	404-032	**ARTURIAN**	8.03	87	13-2	10	GD	R.F.J.Houghton	A.Clark	0-3	
92	1010-04	**SPLICE**	8.11	88	15-2	7	GD-FM	J.Fanshawe	N.Varley	0-2	
93	2400-1	**TRUE PRECISION**	7.10	73	7-1(SF)	3	GD	J.Bethell	L.Charnock	1-1	5f
94	024-1	**TABOOK**	9.05	93	9-2F	6	GD-SFT	A.Scott	B.Raymond	1-1	6f
95	0131-11	**PERRYSTON VIEW**	8.03	81	5-1JF	14	GD-FM	P.Calver	M.Birch	2-2	5f
96	300-122	**ATRAF**	9.07	104	8-1	4	GD-FM	D.Morley	R.Hills	1-3	6f
97	40-4331	**BLUE GOBLIN**	8.13	94	11-10F	10	GD-FM	L.Cumani	L.Dettori	1-4	6f
98	410-104	**MAGIC RAINBOW**	7.13	77	20-1	12	GD-FM	M.Bell	R.Mullen	1-3	6f
99	412-23	**MITCHAM**	9.07	98	9-2	6	GD	T.Mills	Pat Eddery	0-2	

FAVOURITES/SECOND FAVOURITES (strike rate and to a £1 stake): **Favs. 27 per cent, +£2.60,** S.Favs. 8 per cent, -£5.
AVERAGE WINNING RATING: 89.

Introduction

Always a popular betting heat, this has thrown-up Group-class winners like Cadeaux Genereux, Case Law, Splice, Atraf and Blue Goblin.

Ten year analysis

Weight/Rating: Five of the last ten boasted a rating between 93 and 104, while only two scored from marks in the 70s. If pushed, side with a classy horse from the top half of the weights.

Form: Seven won as two-year-olds, none beyond six furlongs. The same number scored earlier in their year, once again all over five or six furlongs. This is not a race for those dropping back in trip. Eight had already run in a handicap as a three-year-old. Be wary of horses coming here on the back of a maiden or conditions-race success.

Latest start: Four won and six were placed on their latest start. A good recent run is vital.

Best trial: The six furlong three-year-old handicap run at Newmarket's Craven Meeting has been an excellent pointer. Five of the last ten ran in that contest, two winning, two making the frame and one finishing unplaced.

CHANTILLY, SUNDAY JUNE 4
PRIX DU JOCKEY-CLUB (GROUP 1) THREE-YEAR-OLD COLTS AND FILLIES (1m 4f)

YR	FORM	WINNER	WT	S.P.	GOING	TRAINER	JOCKEY	RN-WN	FORM IN YEAR WN DIST.
90	2-121	**SANGLAMORE**	9.02	9.5-1	GD-SFT	R.Charlton	Pat Eddery	2-3	10,10f
91	3-112	**SUAVE DANCER**	9.02	3-5F	GD-FM	J.Hammond(FR)	C.Asmussen	2-3	10f
92	-113	**POLYTAIN**	9.02	37-1	GD	A.Spanu(FR)	L.Dettori	2-3	9,10f
93	-2111	**HERNANDO**	9.02	2-1F	GD	F.Boutin(FR)	C.Asmussen	3-4	10f
94	3441-41	**CELTIC ARMS**	9.02	5.3-1	GD-SFT	P.Bary(FR)	G.Mosse	1-2	10f
95	111-12	**CELTIC SWING**	9.02	EV F	GD	Lady Herries	K.Darley	1-2	7f
96	22-1	**RAGMAR**	9.02	9.3-1	FM	P.Bary(FR)	G.Mosse	1-1	10f
97	13-1	**PEINTRE CELEBRE**	9.02	3.1-1F	GD	A.Fabre(FR)	O.Peslier	1-1	10f
98	-221	**DREAM WELL**	9.02	7.8-1	GD	P.Bary(FR)	C.Assmussen	1-3	12f
99	11-12	**MONTJEU**	9.02	1.4-1JF	SFT	J.Hammond	C.Asmussen	1-2	10f

BEST TRIAL: **Prix Greffulhe (Longchamp, April 23)** - five ran: four won, one placed.

Introduction

Although it does not possess the same mystique, the French Derby is a match for its Epsom counterpart in terms of producing quality horses. Winners in the eighties included Assert, Caerleon, Darshaan, Bering and Old Vic, while Suave Dancer, Hernando, Peintre Celebre and Dream Well have scored over the past ten seasons.

Ten year analysis

Form: Winning two-year-old form is not essential - six failed to record a victory at that age - although those who did score won over at least a mile.

Vitally, nine won a Group race earlier in their three-year-old campaign, seven over at least ten furlongs. Only one (Celtic Swing) ran in 'a Guineas', while none were unplaced during their preparation.

Latest start: All ten ran in a Group race on their latest start, five winning and four making the frame.

Best trial: The ten-furlong Prix Greffulhe is our leading trial. Five of the last ten used that event as part of their preparation; Suave Dancer,

Ragmar, Peintre Celebre and Montjeu winning, while Celtic Arms finished fourth.

Betting: Five favourites have won since 1990, which is a decent record.

Top trainers: Pascal Bary has an excellent record in the French Derby, sending out three of the last six winners. John Hammond also deserves a mention after saddling Suave Dancer and Montjeu to score.

EPSOM, FRIDAY JUNE 9
CORONATION CUP (GROUP 1) (1m 4f)

YR	FORM	WINNER	AGE-WT	RATING	S.P.	DRAW	GOING	TRAINER	JOCKEY	FORM IN YEAR WN-RN	WN DIST.
90	11/10-2	**IN THE WINGS**	4 9.00	118	15-8F	4	GD-SFT	A.Fabre(FR)	C.Asmussen	0-1	
91	1301-12	**IN THE GROOVE**	4 8.11	126	7-2	5	GD	D.Elsworth	S.Cauthen	1-2	8f
92	0220-11	**SADDLERS' HALL**	4 9.00	119	5-4F	8	GD	Sir M.Stoute	WR.Swinburn	2-2	12,13f
93	10231-2	**OPERA HOUSE**	5 9.00	123	9-4F	7	GD	Sir M.Stoute	M.Roberts	0-1	
94	0110-42	**APPLE TREE**	5 9.00	120	12-1	10	GD-FM	A.Fabre(FR)	T.Jarnet	0-2	
95	3031-41	**SUNSHACK**	4 9.00	116	10-1	2	GD-FM	A.Fabre(FR)	Pat Eddery	1-2	12f
96	11113-3	**SWAIN**	4 9.00	125	11-10F	2	GD	A.Fabre(FR)	L.Dettori	0-1	
97	21121-1	**SINGSPIEL**	5 9.00	128	5-4F	3	GD	Sir M.Stoute	L.Dettori	1-1	10f
98	12021-2	**SILVER PATRIARCH**	4 9.00	123	7-2(SF)	2	GD	J.Dunlop	Pat Eddery	0-1	
99	1413-02	**DAYLAMI**	5 9.00	123	9-2	3	GD-SFT	S.Bin Suroor	L.Dettori	0-2	

AGE (wins-runners): 4-Y-O: 6-43, 5-Y-O: 4-19, 6-Y-O+: 0-9.

FAVOURITES/SECOND FAVOURITES (strike rate and to a £1 stake): **Favs. 45 per cent, +£1.72, S.Favs.** 8 per cent, -£7.50.

AVERAGE WINNING RATING: 122.

TOP TRAINERS (wins-runners, strike rate and to a £1 stake): **Sir Michael Stoute (3-8, 37 per cent, -£0.25), Andre Fabre (4-10, 40 per cent, +£18.97).**

Introduction

Always hotly contested, this race regularly draws a big name from the other side of the Channel, and has fallen to seven French-trained horses over the past 14 seasons. Keep a close eye on any Gallic raiders making the long journey to Epsom.

Ten year analysis

Age: Five-year-olds have an excellent strike rate, winning four times from just 19 runners since 1990. No horse above the age of five has scored and this is clearly not a race for veterans.

Weight/Rating: As the average win rating of 122 suggests, this race is the preserve of premier league horses. Andre Fabre's shock 10/1 winner Sunshack (116) is the lowest-rated horse on our list, and any entrant running from a lower mark should be avoided.

Form: All ten won a Group race over from 10-12 furlongs during the previous season, confirming that this is a race for proven performers. Each winner had a one or two-race preparation, four scoring and six finishing placed in a Group race. In fact it must be noted that none ran outside Group company earlier in their year.

Latest start: Three won and seven finished placed on their latest start, nine running in a Group One or Two event.

Betting: Favourites have a decent record, winning five of the last ten renewals and producing a small level stakes profit.

Top trainers: Andre Fabre has led the French charge, saddling four winners from ten runners. Those successes have yielded a huge level-stakes profit, and Fabre's entrants are probably worth supporting whatever the Form Book says.
Sir Michael Stoute is only a stride behind in terms of strike rate, his record reading three winners from eight runners since 1990.

EPSOM, FRIDAY JUNE 9
OAKS STAKES (GROUP 1) THREE-YEAR-OLD FILLIES (1m 4f)

										FORM IN YEAR	
YR	FORM	WINNER	WT	RATING	S.P.	DRAW	GOING	TRAINER	JOCKEY	WN-RN	WN DIST.
90	121-11	**SALSABIL**	9.00	-	2-1F	1	GD-SFT	J.Dunlop	W.Carson	2-2	7,8f
91	1310-14	**JET SKI LADY**	9.00	-	50-1	3	GD-FM	J.Bolger(IR)	C.Roche	1-2	10f
92	-11	**USER FRIENDLY**	9.00	-	5-1	5	GD-SFT	C.Brittain	G.Duffield	2-2	10,11.5f
93	1-11	**INTREPIDITY**	9.00	-	5-1(SF)	9	GD-FM	A.Fabre(FR)	M.Roberts	2-2	9,10f
94	11-2	**BALANCHINE**	-	9.00	6-1	9	GD-FM	H.Ibrahim	L.Dettori	0-1	
95	1-3	**MOONSHELL**	-	9.00	3-1(SF)	9	GD-FM	S.Bin Suroor	L.Dettori	0-1	
96	1-1	**LADY CARLA**	-	9.00	10-3(SF)	9	GD	H.Cecil	Pat Eddery	1-1	11.5f
97	2111-01	**REAMS OF VERSE**	119	9.00	5-6F	6	GD	H.Cecil	K.Fallon	1-2	10f
98	241-120	**SHAHTOUSH**	-	9.00	12-1	5	GD	A.O'Brien(IR)	M.Kinane	1-3	8f
99	32-11	**RAMRUMA**	106	9.00	3-1(SF)	5	GD-SFT	H.Cecil	K.Fallon	2-2	11.5, 12f

FAVOURITES/SECOND FAVOURITES (strike rate and to a £1 stake): Favs. 20 per cent, -£5.17, **S.Favs. 40 per cent, +£7.33.**
TOP TRAINERS (wins-runners, strike rate and to a £1 stake): **Henry Cecil (3-8, 37 per cent, +£2.16).**

Introduction

A year older than the Derby, this race has been won by a mixed bag of fillies recently. While Salsabil, User Friendly and Balanchine went on to greater glory, Moonshell, Lady Carla, Reams Of Verse and Shahtoush proved disappointing.

Ten year analysis

Form: Eight won over seven furlongs or a mile as juveniles, only two landing a Group event. Eight went on to score earlier in their three-year-old campaign - nine ran once or twice - three landing Group races and four scoring in Listed company. Avoid fillies that have not been restricted to maiden or minor events.

Latest start: Only one finished unplaced on her latest start, six winning. All ten completed their preparation in Group or Listed races.

Best trials: Five of the last ten ran in the 1000 Guineas at Newmarket, where Salsabil won, Balanchine, Moonshell and Shahtoush made the frame and Reams Of Verse was unplaced. The Lingfield Oaks Trial is also developing into a smart guide. User Friendly, Lady Carla and Ramruma lifted that prize before scoring at Epsom.

Betting: Only two favourites have obliged since 1990 and second favourites have a better record. Look beyond the market leader when making your selection.

Top trainer: Henry Cecil is a master with fillies and has landed this prize three times from just eight runners since 1990. Anything he runs is worth a second glance.

EPSOM, SATURDAY JUNE 10
DERBY STAKES (GROUP 1) THREE-YEAR-OLD COLTS AND FILLIES (1m 4f)

YR	FORM	WINNER	WT	RATING	S.P.	DRAW	GOING	TRAINER	JOCKEY	FORM IN YEAR WN-RN	WN DIST.
90	2-12	**QUEST FOR FAME**	9.00	-	7-1	10	GD-SFT	R.Charlton	Pat Eddery	1-2	11f
91	23011-4	**GENEROUS**	9.00	119	9-1	10	GD-FM	P.Cole	A.Munro	0-1	
92	1121-20	**DR DEVIOUS**	9.00	113	8-1(SF)	4	GD	P.Chapple-Hyam	J.Reid	0-2	
93	-111	**COMMANDER IN CHIEF**	9.00	111	15-2(SF)	6	GD	H.Cecil	M.Kinane	3-3	10,12f
94	1123-21	**ERHAAB**	9.00	120	7-2F	15	GD	J.Dunlop	W.Carson	1-2	10f

95	1-	**LAMMTARRA**	9.00	-	14-1	7	FM	S.Bin Suroor	W.Swinburn	0-0	
96	41-	**SHAAMIT**	9.00	-	12-1	9	GD	W.Haggas	M.Hills	0-0	
97	1113-21	**BENNY THE DIP**	9.00	119	11-1	8	GD	J.Gosden	W.Ryan	1-2	10f
98	1-11	**HIGH-RISE**	9.00	112	20-1	14	GD	L.Cumani	O.Peslier	2-2	10,11.5f
99	031-21	**OATH**	9.00	117	13-2(SF)	1	GD	H.Cecil	K.Fallon	1-2	10f

FAVOURITES/SECOND FAVOURITES (strike rate and to a £1 stake): Favs. 9 per cent, -£6.50, **S.Favs. 27 per cent, +£14.**
AVERAGE WINNING RATING: 116.

Introduction

Fashions come and go, but Epsom's Derby remains the focal point of the domestic season. That said, several recent winners could be regarded as sub-standard, and the race needs the shot in the arm that only an outstanding performance can bring.

Ten year analysis

Weight/Rating: Seven of the last ten had a rating coming into the race, their marks ranging from 111 (Commander in Chief) to 120 (Erhaab).

Draw: Winners have come from every type of draw, and more importance should be placed on the ability to grab a decent position from an early stage.

Form: Nine ran as two-year-olds, eight winning over seven furlongs or a mile, seven from September. Note that only three landed a Group race during their first season.
Eight ran earlier in their year (only one more than twice), six winning. It is vital to remember that only one (Generous) took part in the 2000 Guineas.
Finally, only five had won a Group race earlier in their career and your selection need not be proven in that grade.

Latest Start: Seven of the last ten came into the Derby on the back of a confidence-boosting win, while only mould-breaking Dr Devious had finished unplaced. It should also be pointed out that seven completed their preparation by running over 10-12 furlongs.

Betting: Erhaab is the only winning favourite since 1990. However, second favourites have fared better, scoring on three occasions and recording a healthy level-stakes profit.

Top trainers: There are no outstanding training trends, although it should be noted that the Derby has not been won by an Irish horse since David O'Brien's Secreto in 1984.
Worse still, the French have drawn a blank for almost a quarter-century, Maurice Zilber's Empery (1976) being their last scorer.

YORK, SATURDAY JUNE 17
WILLIAM HILL TROPHY HANDICAP (0-105) THREE-YEAR-OLDS (6f)

YR	FORM	WINNER	WT	RATING	S.P	DRAW	GOING	TRAINER	JOCKEY	FORM IN YR WN-RN	WN DIST.
90	222-131	**KATZAKEENA**	8.10	94	7-2f	1	GD-FM	P.Makin	B.Raymond	2-3	5,6f
91	0-12	**SHEIKH ALBADOU**	9.03	102	9-4f	1	GD	A.Scott	Pat Eddery	1-2	6f
92	23-0010	**OTHORHOMBUS**	9.02	96	15-2	1	FM	G.Lewis	Paul Eddery	1-4	6f
93	0-44300	**ARADANZA**	9.02	94	25-1	6	GD-SFT	M.Channon	Paul Eddery	0-5	
94	23-142	**ENCORE M'LADY**	7.11	76	20-1	14	GD-FM	F.Lee	N.Carlisle	1-3	5f
95	100132	**BOLD EFFORT**	8.08	87	10-1	4	GD-FM	K.C'ham-Brown	T.Ives	3-9	6f
96	431-02	**MALLIA**	7.10	79	14-1	17	GD	T.D.Barron	L.Charnock	0-2	
97	1-42400	**RETURN OF AMIN**	7.07	71	11-1	7	GD-SFT	J.Bethell	P.Fessey	0-5	
98	3340-20	**FRIAR TUCK**	8.11	95	33-1	15	GD-SFT	L.Perratt	J.Weaver	0-2	
99	001-202	**PEPPERDINE**	8.03	85	10-1	17	GD-SFT	D.Nicholls	G.Carter	0-3	

FAVOURITES/SECOND FAVOURITES (strike rate and to a £1 stake): **Favs. 20 per cent, -£2.25,** S.Favs. 0 per cent, -£11.
AVERAGE WINNING RATING: 88.

Introduction

This, one of the season's top three-year-old sprint handicaps, numbers Governor General, Dowsing, Cadeaux Genereux and Sheikh Albadou among its old boys. That quartet developed into Group horses and their successor is worth following.

Ten year analysis

Weight/Rating: This was dominated by horses with high ratings in the early nineties. However, only one of the last six winners was rated above 87 so it could pay to look lower down the scale when making your choice.

Form: No maiden has scored, but it is inconsequential whether that win came at two or three. More importance should be placed on the fact that nine had their latest start in a handicap from May. Avoid any who have been restricted to maiden or minor events.

Latest start: Only one last start winner has scored since 1990. Look for a horse that escaped the Handicapper's attention on his latest outing.

Betting: This is a desperate race for market leaders. No favourite has scored since 1991, while second favourites have drawn a blank over the past decade.

ROYAL ASCOT, TUESDAY JUNE 20
QUEEN ANNE STAKES (GROUP 2) (1m)

YR	FORM	WINNER	AGE-WT	RATING	S.P	DRAW	GOING	TRAINER	JOCKEY	FORM IN YR WNS-RNS	WN DIST.
90	1323-14	**MARKOFDISTINCTION**	4 9.05	120	7-1	7	GD-FM	L.Cumani	L.Dettori	1-2	8f
91	31-2410	**SIKESTON**	5 9.08	121	9-1	10	GD	C.Brittain	M.Roberts	1-4	10f
92	21-02	**LAHIB**	4 9.02	-	100-30F	5	GD-FM	J.Dunlop	W.Carson	0-2	
93	243-241	**ALFLORA**	4 9.02	111	20-1	6	GD-SFT	C.Brittain	M.Kinane	1-3	7f
94	100420-	**BARATHEA**	4 9.08	123	3-1(SF)	1	GD-FM	L.Cumani	M.Kinane	0-0	
95	23/4-423	**NICOLOTTE**	4 9.02	110	16-1	2	GD-FM	G.Wragg	M.Hills	0-3	
96	2/121-2	**CHARNWOOD FOREST**	4 9.02	119	10-11F	6	GD-FM	S.Bin Suroor	M.Kinane	0-1	
97	100011-	**ALLIED FORCES**	4 9.05	-	10-1	11	GD	S.Bin Suroor	L.Dettori	0-0	
98	111-121	**INTIKHAB**	4 9.02	111	9-4F	6	GD-SFT	S.Bin Suroor	L.Dettori	2-3	8,9f
99	10340-3	**CAPE CROSS**	5 9.07	120	7-1	2	GD-FM	S.Bin Suroor	G.Stevens	0-1	

AGE (wins-runners): 3-Y-O: 0-7, 4-Y-O: 8-59, 5-Y-O: 2-15, 6-Y-O+: 0-11.
FAVOURITES/SECOND FAVOURITES (strike rate and to a £1 stake): **Favs. 27 per cent, -£1.51,** S.Favs. 8 per cent, -£8.
AVERAGE WINNING RATING: 117.
TOP TRAINER (wins-runs, strike rate and to a £1 stake): Saeed Bin Suroor (4-7, 57 per cent, +£17.16).

Introduction

Royal Ascot's curtain raiser, this contest usually helps finalise the pecking order among the best of our older milers. Outstanding horses like Markofdistinction, Barathea and Intikhab figure among the recent winners and this is no place for those lacking class.

Ten year analysis

Age: Four-year-olds dominate in terms of runners and winners, scoring eight times from 59 entrants since 1990. Five-year-olds also have a fair record, although three-year-olds and those aged six or above should be avoided.

Weight/Rating: Relatively lowly rated horses like Alflora (111), Nicolotte (110) and Intikhab (111) have won recently. Do not be afraid to support an improver.

Form: Eight won in the season before they landed this event, but only four scored during their preparation. Look beyond the obvious when making your selection.

Latest start: Eight ran earlier in their year, six taking part in a Group race on their latest start (one won, four placed and one was unplaced).

Best trial: Newbury's Lockinge Stakes (run on May 20) is usually a useful pointer. Four of the last ten ran in that event, two finishing second and two fourth.

Betting: There have been a few surprise results over the past decade, leaving both favourites and second favourites showing a level-stakes loss.

Top trainer: Saeed Bin Suroor and the Godolphin team have made this race their own, winning the last four runnings. That adds up to a healthy level-stakes profit and the message to backers is clear - if in doubt, follow the boys-in-blue.

ROYAL ASCOT, TUESDAY JUNE 20
PRINCE OF WALES'S STAKES (GROUP 2) (1m 2f)

YR	FORM	WINNER	AGE-WT	RATING	S.P	DRAW	GOING	TRAINER	JOCKEY	FORM IN YEAR WN-RN	WN DIST.
90	303-131	**BATSHOOF**	4 9.05	-	2-1F	3	GD-FM	B.Hanbury	Pat Eddery	2-3	10f
91	2/311-1	**STAGECRAFT**	4 9.03	-	6-4F	4	GD	Sir M.Stoute	S.Cauthen	1-1	10f
92	1/131-4	**PERPENDICULAR**	4 9.03	112	20-1	10	GD-FM	H.Cecil	W.Ryan	0-1	
93	1-120	**PLACERVILLE**	3 8.04	110	11-2	1	GD-SFT	H.Cecil	Pat Eddery	1-3	9f
94	1110-12	**MUHTARRAM**	5 9.07	116	6-4F	8	GD-FM	J.Gosden	W.Carson	1-2	10f
95	22343-0	**MUHTARRAM**	6 9.08	123	5-1	5	GD-FM	J.Gosden	W.Carson	0-1	
96	02-1301	**FIRST ISLAND**	4 9.03	114	9-1	3	GD-FM	G.Wragg	M.Hills	2-4	8f
97	1/1121-1	**BOSRA SHAM**	4 9.05	131	4-11F	1	GD	H.Cecil	K.Fallon	1-1	10f
98	12013-1	**FAITHFUL SON**	4 9.03	115	11-2(SF)	7	GD-SFT	S.bin Suroor	J.Reid	1-1	10f
99	14-0401	**LEAR SPEAR**	4 9.03	109	20-1	5	GD-FM	D.Elsworth	M.Kinane	1-4	8.5f

AGE (wins-runners): 3-Y-O: 1-12, 4-Y-O: 7-55, 5-Y-O: 1-12, 6-Y-O+: 1-8.
FAVOURITES/SECOND FAVOURITES (strike rate and to a £1 stake): **Favs. 33 per cent, -£2.64**, S.Favs. 7 per cent, -£8.50.
AVERAGE WINNING RATING: 116.
TOP TRAINER (wins-runners, strike rate and to a £1 stake): **Henry Cecil (3-10, 30 per cent, +£18.86).**

Introduction

This ten-furlong contest has been won by a mixed bag of horses over the past two decades. In the plus column we have outstanding performers like Stanerra, Mtoto and Bosra Sham, in the debit instantly forgettable horses such as Morcon, English Spring, Two Timing and Perpendicular. As those lists suggest, this is a race where 'shock' results are relatively commonplace.

Ten year analysis

Age: This is definitely a four-year-olds race. They have won the last four renewals, bringing their ten-year total to seven.

Weight/Rating: Six were rated between 109 and 116, which is a relatively low mark for a contest of this stature.

Form: Eight won during their preparation, seven landing a Group or Listed contest (five over ten furlongs). Note that two won and three were placed in a ten-furlong Group race at Sandown earlier in their year.

Latest start: Six won on their latest start, although it is probably more important to remember that eight completed their preparation by running in a Group race.

Betting: Favourites and second favourites have produced a level-stakes loss since 1990. There have been two 20/1 winners during this period and outsiders have every chance.

Top trainer: Henry Cecil's three winners from ten runners have yielded a huge level-stakes profit (£18.86). While that figure is exaggerated slightly by Perpendicular's 20/1 surprise, his runners must be treated with plenty of respect.

ROYAL ASCOT, TUESDAY JUNE 20
ST JAMES'S PALACE STAKES (GROUP 1) THREE-YEAR-OLDS (1m)

YR	FORM	WINNER	WT	RATING	S.P	DRAW	GOING	TRAINER	JOCKEY	FORM IN YEAR WN-RN	WN DIST.
90	21-34	**SHAVIAN**	9.00		11-1	4	GD-FM	H.Cecil	S.Cauthen	0-2	
91	1-102	**MARJU**	9.00		7-4F	5	GD	J.Dunlop	W.Carson	1-3	8f
92	1-2131	**BRIEF TRUCE**	9.00	-	25-1	2	GD-FM	D.Weld(IR)	M.Kinane	2-4	8,10f
93	0202-11	**KINGMAMBO**	9.00	-	2-5F	4	GD-SFT	F.Boutin(FR)	C.Asmussen	2-2	7,8f
94	311-024	**GRAND LODGE**	9.00	120	6-1	3	GD-FM	W.Jarvis	M.Kinane	0-3	
95	221-233	**BAHRI**	9.00	125	11-4F	7	GD-FM	J.Dunlop	W.Carson	0-3	
96	2110-34	**BIJOU D'INDE**	9.00	120	9-1	7	GD-FM	M.Johnston	J.Weaver	0-2	
97	134-141	**STARBOROUGH**	9.00	119	11-2	5	GD	D.Loder	L.Dettori	2-3	8,9f

98	11-143	**DR FONG**	9.00	114	4-1(SF)	4	GD-SFT	H.Cecil	K.Fallon	1-3	10f
99	22-121	**SENDAWAR**	9.00	-	2-1F	11	GD-FM	A.deRoyer-Dupre	G.Mosse	2-3	8,10f

FAVOURITES/SECOND FAVOURITES (strike rate and to a £1 stake): **Favs. 40 per cent, +£0.90,** S.Favs. 8 per cent, -£7.
AVERAGE WINNING RATING: 120.

Introduction

One of the hottest mile races of the year, this event figures as one leg of Ascot's 'Millennium Million Miler Challenge'. To be eligible for that £1 million bonus, the colt in question must complete an unprecedented hat-trick by winning the Royal Lodge Stakes, St James's Palace Stakes and Queen Elizabeth II Stakes.

Ten year analysis

Weight/Rating: As is borne out by an average win rating of 120, this is a race for proven horses.

Form: Nine won as two-year-olds, only two in Group events. A three-year-old win is less important, although it is vital to note that eight ran in 'a Guineas' during their preparation, two winning and five making the frame.

Latest start: Eight ran in a Group One on their latest start, three winning and five making the frame. Avoid any taking a big step-up in class.

Best trial: The English 2000 Guineas has been the best trial. Five of the last ten ran there, Grand Lodge, Bahri, Bijou D'Inde and Starborough making the frame while Marju was unplaced. Second best is the Irish 2000 Guineas, where four ran, each making the frame. Note that three made the frame in both races.

Betting: Favourites have a fair record, 40 per cent winning since 1990. Second favourites have been less successful and show a heavy level-stakes loss.

ROYAL ASCOT, TUESDAY JUNE 20
COVENTRY STAKES (GROUP 3) TWO-YEAR-OLDS (6f)

YR	FORM	WINNER	WT	S.P	DRAW	GOING	TRAINER	JOCKEY	FORM IN YEAR WN-RN	WN DIST.
90	2111	**MAC'S IMP**	8.13	2-1F	8	GD-FM	W.O'Gorman	A.Munro	3-4	5,6f

91	21	**DILUM**	8.13	11-10F	6	GD	P.Cole	A.Munro	1-2	6f
92	1	**PETARDIA**	8.13	5-1JF	1	GD-FM	G.Wragg	W.Swinburn	1-1	5f
93	1	**STONEHATCH**	8.13	EV F	5	GD-SFT	P.Chapple-Hyam	J.Reid	1-1	6f
94	211	**SRI PEKAN**	8.13	6-1	14	GD-FM	P.Cole	T.Quinn	2-3	5,6f
95	1	**ROYAL APPLAUSE**	8.12	13-2(SF)	12	GD-FM	B.Hills	W.Swinburn	1-1	5f
96	31	**VERGLAS**	8.12	9-1	3	GD-FM	K.Predergast(IR)	W.Supple	1-2	6f
97	10	**HARBOUR MASTER**	8.12	16-1	3	GD	A.O'Brien(IR)	C.Roche	1-2	5f
98	1	**RED SEA**	8.12	6-1(SF)	19	GD-SFT	P.Cole	T.Quinn	1-1	6f
99	11	**FASLIYEV**	8.12	15-8F	17	GD-FM	A.O'Brien(IR)	M.Kinane	2-2	5f

FAVOURITES/SECOND FAVOURITES (strike rate and to a £1 stake): Favs. 38 per cent, +£2.97, **S.Favs. 18 per cent, +£3.50.**
TOP TRAINER (wins-runs, strike rate and to a £1 stake): **Paul Cole (3-7, 43 per cent, +£9.10).**

Introduction

This race has launched some phenomenal careers, including those of Mill Reef and Chief Singer. However, not all the winners train on, High Estate, Mac's Imp and Dilum being three recent high-profile flops.

Ten year analysis

Draw: Winners have come from both sides of the track in recent years and the draw does not seem of any great consequence.

Form: Avoid over-exposed precocious types – eight had a maximum of two starts beforehand. All ten boasted winning form, only two finishing out of the first two during their preparation.

Latest start: Nine of the last ten won from May on their latest start. Any failing to meet this criterion should be ignored.

Betting: Favourites and second favourites show a level-stakes profit since 1990. The market is usually a solid guide.

Top trainers: Paul Cole has run seven horses here during the past decade, producing three winners and two placed horses. Anything from his yard is worth a second glance.
Aidan O'Brien has also shown a liking for the race, sending out Harbour Master and Fasliyev to win in the past three seasons. The young master of Ballydoyle could make this race his own.

ROYAL ASCOT, TUESDAY JUNE 20
BRITANNIA HANDICAP (0-105) THREE-YEAR-OLDS (1m)

YR FORM	WINNER	WT	RATING	S.P	DRAW	GOING	TRAINER	JOCKEY	FORM IN YEAR WN-RN	WN DIST.
90 010-00	**FOX CHAPEL**	7.07	81	100-1	20	GD-SFT	R.Hannon	G.Hind	0-2	
91 -21	**AJAAD**	9.00	94	12-1	21	GD	M.Stoute	B.Raymond	1-2	7f
92 040-021	**EFHARISTO**	8.00	79	14-1	2	GD-FM	C.Brittain	M.Roberts	1-3	7f
93 4302-21	**SHOW FAITH**	8.05	84	6-1F	20	SFT	R.Hannon	Pat Eddery	1-2	8f
94 12-3121	**WIZARD KING**	7.07	77	9-1(SF)	28	GD-FM	Sir M.Prescott	J.Lowe	2-4	7f
95 03-1	**MEDAILLE MILITAIRE**	8.03	84	4-1F	10	GD-FM	J.Dunlop	T.Quinn	1-1	8f
96 -221	**NORTH SONG**	8.01	84	14-1	23	GD-FM	J.Gosden	G.Hind	1-3	9f
97 32-1204	**FLY TO THE STARS**	9.03	100	20-1	14	GD	M.Johnston	O.Peslier	1-4	8f
98 02-03	**PLAN-B**	8.07	88	8-1(SF)	30	GD-SFT	J.Gosden	L.Dettori	0-2	
99 0-13	**PYTHIOS**	9.00	92	10-1JF	1	GD-FM	H.Cecil	K.Fallon	1-2	7f

FAVOURITES/SECOND FAVOURITES (strike rate and to a £1 stake): **Favs. 21 per cent, +£9, S.Favs. 20 per cent, +£9.**
AVERAGE WINNING RATING: 86.

Introduction

This is often won by a horse with the scope to hold his own in Group company. For example, Protection (1985), Foreign Survivor (1988), Wizard King (1994) and Fly To The Stars (1997) all made the jump out of handicaps into Pattern events.

Ten year analysis

Weight/Rating: Only three of the last ten carried above 8st 7lbs – this is hard to win under a big weight. Similarly, Ajaad, Fly To The Stars and Pythios are the only recent scorers rated above 88 – look for something around our average win rating of 86.

Draw: Winners have come from both sides of the track, although it could be worth noting that six of the last ten were drawn in stalls 20-30.

Form: You need a few pounds in hand to win a race of this type, so stick with 'unexposed' horses when making your selection. Only two of the last ten scored as juveniles, eight having a maximum of three starts at that age.
Eight won earlier in their year, seven over seven furlongs or a mile, six from May. Only two had run in more than a single handicap, underlining the 'unexposed' feel of the race.

Latest start: Six won and three finished placed on their latest start – avoid any that disappointed last time.

Betting: While this looks a potential nightmare for punters, both first and second favourites show a level-stakes profit since 1990.

Top trainers: There are no outstanding training trends, although John Gosden (two winners and three placed) and Richard Hannon (two winners and four placed) have decent records.

ROYAL ASCOT. TUESDAY JUNE 20
ASCOT HANDICAP £46,000 (2m 4f)

YR	FORM	WINNER	AGE-WT	RATING	S.P	DRAW	GOING	TRAINER	JOCKEY	FORM IN YEAR WN-RN	WN DIST.
90	1230-42	**RETOUCH**	4 8.02	84	12-1	17	GD-FM	P.Cole	M.Roberts	0-2	
91	211-030	**CABOCHON**	4 8.06	71	15-2	9	GD	D.Morley	W.Carson	0-3	
92	041-034	**GONDOLIER**	4 9.09	86	7-1F	3	GD-FM	H.Cecil	Pat Eddery	0-3	
93	1113/41	**BALASANI**	7 9.01	75	8-1(SF)	14	GD-SFT	M.Pipe	M.Perrett	1-2	14f
94	0//00-000	**SWEET GLOW**	7 9.01	71	14-1	14	GD-FM	M.Pipe	C.Asmussen	0-3	
95	1100-02	**HARLESTONE BROOK**	5 9.08	84	6-1(SF)	7	GD-FM	J.Dunlop	M.Kinane	0-2	
96	23423-3	**SOUTHERN POWER**	5 9.07	79	25-1	9	GD-FM	R.Akehurst	O.Peslier	0-1	
97	011243	**SEA FREEDOM**	6 8.03	65	20-1	24	GD	G.Balding	S.Drowne	2-6	13,14f
98	112-221	**SAN SEBASTIAN**	4 9.05	84	16-1	8	GD-SFT	M.Grassick(IR)	E.Ahern	1-3	14f
99	331-204	**HIGH AND MIGHTY**	4 9.06	85	10-1(SF)	20	GD-FM	J.Gosden	L.Dettori	0-3	

AGE (wins-runners): 4-Y-O: 5-103, 5-Y-O: 2-63, 6-Y-O+: 3-79.
FAVOURITES/SECOND FAVOURITES (strike rate and to a £1 stake): Favs. 9 per cent, -£3.00, **S.Favs. 30 per cent, +£17.**
AVERAGE WINNING RATING: 78.

Introduction

A gruelling test of stamina, this race usually attracts a mixed bag of runners, ranging from smart handicappers to moderate chasers and hurdlers.

Ten year analysis

Age: Four-year-olds have the best strike rate, but age is not a significant factor.

Weight/Rating: This is a high-weights race. Seven of the last ten carried a minimum of 9st 1lb.

Form: Possibly the most interesting form pointer is that only one ran more than three times during his preparation.
A recent win is certainly not essential – seven failed to score beforehand – although six did manage to make the frame in a handicap over at least two miles in May.

Latest start: Nine had their latest start in a handicap during May, only one winning while six made the frame.

Betting: Favourites have a modest record, but second favourites have provided plenty of relief for punters, winning three times at a decent level stakes profit since 1990.

Top trainer: Martin Pipe always likes to lay something out for this race and has saddled two winners and four placed horses over the past decade.

ROYAL ASCOT, WEDNESDAY JUNE 21
JERSEY STAKES THREE-YEAR-OLDS (7f)

YR	FORM	WINNER	WT	RATING	S.P	DRAW	GOING	TRAINER	JOCKEY	FORM IN YEAR WN-RN	WN DIST.
90	1-400	SALLY ROUS	8.07	-	20-1	3	FM	G.Wragg	G.Carter	0-3	
91	-12	SATIN FLOWER	8.07	98	12-1	12	GD	J.Gosden	S.Cauthen	1-2	8f
92	222-111	PRINCE FERDINAND	9.01	117	6-1(SF)	8	GD-FM	M.McCormack	J.Reid	3-3	6,7f
93	1411-03	ARDKINGLASS	9.01	116	10-1	8	SFT	H.Cecil	W.Ryan	0-2	
*94	210-010	GNEISS	8.10	108	10-1	4	GD-FM	J.Cecil	Paul Eddery	1-3	8f
	20-1003	RIVER DEEP	8.10	109	20-1	1	GD-FM	P.Cole	T.Quinn	1-4	7f
95	130-111	SERGEYEV	8.10	112	5-1F	5	GD-FM	R.Hannon	R.Hughes	3-3	6,7f
96	12-032	LUCAYAN PRINCE	8.10	97	50-1	2	GD-FM	D.Loder	R.Hughes	0-3	
97	-11	AMONG MEN	8.13	-	4-1F	13	GD-FM	M.Stoute	M.Kinane	2-2	8f
98	0-11	DIKTAT	8.10	113	3-1F	2	GD-SFT	D.Loder	D.Holland	2-2	7f
99	2414-14	LOTS OF MAGIC	8.11	100	33-1	3	GD-FM	R.Hannon	D.O'Neill	1-2	7f

* Dead-heat

FAVOURITES/SECOND FAVOURITES (strike rate and to a £1 stake): **Favs. 27 per cent,** +£4, S.Favs. 9 per cent, -£4.
AVERAGE WINNING RATING: 108.

Introduction

Restricted to those who have not won a Group One or Two, this has fallen to embryonic stars like Zilzal, Sally Rous, Lucayan Prince, Among Men and Diktat in recent years. Their successor could easily go on to bigger and better things.

Ten year analysis

Weight/Rating: No horse has defied a Group Three penalty for over 30 years, so avoid any carrying that burden.

Several recent winners – Satin Flower, Lucayan Prince and Lots Of Magic for example – were rated no better than run-of-the-mill performers when scoring, so your selection need not be an established star.

Draw: Seven came from stalls numbered 1-5. Those drawn on the stands' side might have a slight advantage.

Form: Seven won as two-year-olds, only one making the frame in Group company. Eight scored earlier in their year, each landing a non-handicap over seven furlongs or a mile.
Only two won a Listed race earlier in their year, while Sally Rous was the only entrant to make the frame in a Group race (she finished fourth in the Nell Gwyn Stakes). This is definitely a race for those who have been competing away from the spot-light.

Latest start: Only two ran over this seven-furlong trip on their latest start, seven completing their preparation over a mile or beyond. Keep an eye on those dropping back in distance.

Betting: Favourites have produced a handy level-stakes profit but, as Sally Rous, River Deep, Lucayan Prince and Lots Of Magic have shown, this is a race where shock results can occur.

ROYAL ASCOT, WEDNESDAY JUNE 21
QUEEN MARY STAKES (GROUP 3) TWO-YEAR-OLD FILLIES (5f)

YR	FORM	WINNER	WT	S.P	DRAW	GOING	TRAINER	JOCKEY	FORM IN YEAR WN-RN	WN DIST.
90	11	**ON TIPTOES**	8.08	8-1	2	FM	J.Leigh	D.Mckeown	2-2	5f
91	11	**MARLING**	8.08	11-4F	11	GD	G.Wragg	G.Carter	2-2	5f
92	11	**LYRIC FANTASY**	8.08	11-8F	10	GD-FM	R.Hannon	M.Roberts	2-2	5f
93	112	**RISKY**	8.08	11-2	6	SFT	R.Hannon	W.Swinburn	2-3	5f
94	0	**GAY GALLANTA**	8.08	16-1	16	GD-FM	Sir M.Stoute	W.Swinburn	0-1	
95	1	**BLUE DUSTER**	8.08	7-4F	10	GD-FM	D.Loder	M.Kinane	1-1	5f0
96	11	**DANCE PARADE**	8.08	8-1	2	GD-FM	P.Cole	M.Kinane	2-2	5f
97	13	**NADWAH**	8.08	10-1	1	GD-FM	P.Walwyn	R.Hills	1-2	5f
98	21	**BINT ALLAYL**	8.08	2-1F	5	GD-SFT	M.Channon	L.Dettori	1-2	5f
99	21	**SHINING HOUR**	8.08	20-1	3	GD-FM	P.Chapple-Hyam	J.Fortune	1-2	5.5f

FAVOURITES/SECOND FAVOURITES (strike rate and to a £1 stake): **Favs. 40 per cent, +£1.87,** S.Favs. 0 per cent, -£11.
RACE RECORD: Marling, Lyric Fantasy, Gay Gallanta and Blue Duster went on to win the Group 1 Cheveley Park Stakes. It could be worth supporting this year's Queen Mary heroine if she takes her chance in that championship event.

Introduction

This is more than just a race for precocious juveniles: Marling, Lyric Fantasy, Gay Gallanta and Blue Duster went on to win the Group One Cheveley Park Stakes, and it would be no surprise if their successor graduated to bigger and better things.

Ten year analysis

Form: Only Gay Gallanta failed to score beforehand. The remainder all won from May, none beyond an extended five furlongs. Only one ran more than twice or finished unplaced during her preparation.

Latest start: Seven won their latest start. Stick with recent scorers when making your selection.

Best trial: Sandown Park's National Stakes – a Listed event run in late May – has been a fine guide. Five of the last ten ran in that contest, Marling, Lyric Fantasy and Bint Allayl winning, while Risky and Nadwah finished third.

Betting: Favourites have produced a 40 per cent strike rate and useful level-stakes profit since 1990. Second favourites have been wholly unsuccessful during the same period, failing to register a success.

Top trainers: No outstanding records, although Richard Hannon has saddled two winners and two placed fillies since 1990.
It is also worth noting that Mick Channon has produced a winner and second-placed runner in the past two seasons. A noted handler of juveniles, he is a trainer to watch here.

ROYAL ASCOT, WEDNESDAY JUNE 21
CORONATION STAKES (GROUP 1) THREE-YEAR-OLD FILLIES (1m)

YR	FORM	WINNER	WT	RATING	S.P	DRAW	GOING	TRAINER	JOCKEY	FORM IN YEAR WN-RN	WN DIST.
90	11113-4	**CHIMES OF FREEDOM**	9.00	112	11-2	4	FM	H.Cecil	S.Cauthen	0-1	
91	121-121	**KOOYONGA**	9.00	-	3-1(SF)	4	GD	M.Kauntze(IR)	W.O'Connor	2-3	7,8f
92	1111-21	**MARLING**	9.00	118	8-11F	7	GD-FM	G.Wragg	W.Swinburn	1-2	8f
93	241-23	**GOLD SPLASH**	9.00	113	10-3(SF)	2	SFT	C.Head(FR)	G.Mosse	0-2	
94	1230-01	**KISSING COUSIN**	9.00	107	13-2	2	GD-FM	H.Cecil	M.Kinane	1-2	7f
95	31-11	**RIDGEWOOD PEARL**	9.00	-	9-2(SF)	8	GD-FM	J.Oxx(IR)	J.Murtagh	2-2	7,8f
96	4012-12	**SHAKE THE YOKE**	9.00	114	EV F	4	GD-FM	E.Lellouche(FR)	O.Peslier	1-2	8f
97	2-10	**REBECCA SHARP**	9.00	94	25-1	3	GD-FM	G.Wragg	M.Hills	1-2	7f
98	13-03	**EXCLUSIVE**	9.00	110	5-1(SF)	10	GD-SFT	Sir M.Stoute	W.Swinburn	0-2	
99	231-2	**BALISADA**	9.00	100	16-1	8	GD-FM	G.Wragg	M.Roberts	0-1	

FAVOURITES/SECOND FAVOURITES (strike rate and to a £1 stake): Favs. 20 per cent, -£6.27, **S.Favs. 36 per cent, +£8.83.**
AVERAGE WINNING RATING: 108.
TOP TRAINER (wins-runs, strike rate and to a £1 stake): **Geoff Wragg (3-5, 60 per cent, +£39.73).**

Introduction

Although prone to shock results, this always falls to a top-class filly, numbering Kooyonga, Marling and Ridgewood Pearl among its winners. That trio went on to beat the colts, and their successor may follow suit.

Ten year analysis

Weight/Rating: The average win rating of 108 is tame for a Group One. This can fall to a progressive filly who has yet to prove herself in the top-class.

Form: Six won and two made the frame in a Group race as two-year-olds. Winning three-year-old form is not essential (four failed to score), although it is worth noting that seven ran in a mile Classic during their preparation, three winning and three making the frame.

Latest start: Seven ran in a mile Classic last time, three winning, three making the frame and one finishing unplaced.

Best trial: The English 1000 Guineas is our best trial. Four of the last ten ran in that Classic, Kooyonga, Marling and Exclusive making the frame, while Rebecca Sharp was unplaced.

Betting: Favourites have a poor record, but second favourites have produced a decent level-stakes profit over the past decade. Look beyond the market leader.

Top trainer: Geoff Wragg has a remarkable record, producing three winners from just five runners since 1990. Two of those - Rebecca Sharp and Balisada – were well backed at long odds, and it could pay to look for similarly inspired moves from this shrewd yard in the future.

ROYAL ASCOT, WEDNESDAY JUNE 21
ROYAL HUNT CUP (HANDICAP) £120,000 (1m)

YR	FORM	WINNER	AGE-WT	RATING	S.P	DRAW	GOING	TRAINER	JOCKEY	FORM IN YEAR WN-RN	WN DIST.
90	30/00-10	PONTENUOVO	5 7.07	75	50-1	4	FM	D.Elsworth	G.Bardwell	1-2	9f
91	14100-0	EUROLINK THE LAD	4 8.09	89	25-1	30	GD	J.Dunlop	J.Reid	0-1	

92 001300-	**COLOUR SERGEANT**	4 7.13	78	20-1	11	GD-FM	Ld Huntingdon	D.Harrison	0-0	
93 0/110-10	**IMPERIAL BALLET**	4 8.12	98	20-1	19	SFT	H.Cecil	Pat Eddery	1-2	8f
94 2004-01	**FACE NORTH**	6 8.03	83	25-1	30	GD-FM	R.Akehurst	A.Munro	1-2	7f
95 12-0002	**REALITIES**	5 9.00	99	11-1(SF)	30	GD-FM	G.Harwood	M.Kinane	0-4	
96 032-112	**YEAST**	4 8.06	87	8-1F	3	GD-FM	W.Haggas	K.Fallon	2-3	7,8f
97 10/30-0	**RED ROBBO**	4 8.06	88	16-1	17	GD-FM	R.Akehurst	O.Peslier	0-1	
98 422142	**REFUSE TO LOSE**	4 7.11	83	20-1	6	GD-SFT	J.Eustace	J.Tate	2-7	8f
99 00-1023	**SHOWBOAT**	5 8.06	92	14-1	30	GD-FM	B.Hills	N.Pollard	1-4	7f

AGE (wins-runners): 3-Y-O: 0-4, 4-Y-O: 6-165, 5-Y-O: 3-85, 6-Y-O+: 1-59.
FAVOURITES/SECOND FAVOURITES (strike rate and to a £1 stake): **Favs. 9 per cent, -£2**, S.Favs. 7 per cent, -£2.
AVERAGE WINNING RATING: 87.

Introduction

Run over a straight mile at a breakneck gallop, this is one of Flat racing's most competitive and prestigious handicaps. While none of the recent winners were Group class, several – Imperial Ballet, Realities, Yeast and Refuse To Lose – were close to that level. This is a race for above-average performers.

Ten year analysis

Age: Three-year-olds must be avoided (they are better employed in Tuesday's Britannia Handicap), and this is best left to four and five-year-olds, who boast almost identical strike rates.

Weight/Rating: None of the last ten winners carried more than 9st. Those at the head of the weights obviously face a tough task.

Draw: Winners have come from every side of the track, although it is worth noting that four of the last ten were sited in stall 30. While some pundits fear a high draw over the straight course at Ascot, results suggest it is no bar to success.

Form: Perhaps the most interesting form pointer is that only Refuse To Lose ran more than four times during his preparation. This is best left to those who have been laid-out for the race.

Latest start: Only Face North won on his latest start. Look for a horse that is about to peak, rather than one sustaining a high.

Best trial: The Victoria Cup Handicap – run over seven furlongs on this track in late April – has been a fair guide. Four of the last ten ran in that contest, Face North and Yeast winning, while Realities and Showboat finished out of the money.

Betting: Both favourites and second favourites have registered a single success since 1990. Look for some value just beyond the market leaders.

ROYAL ASCOT, WEDNESDAY JUNE 21
QUEEN'S VASE (GROUP 3) THREE-YEAR-OLDS (2m)

YR	FORM	WINNER	WT	RATING	S.P	DRAW	GOING	TRAINER	JOCKEY	FORM IN YEAR WNS-RNS	WN DIST.
90	3-10	**RIVER GOD**	8.11	-	6-4F	11	FM	H.Cecil	S.Cauthen	1-2	12f
91	4-2	**JENDALI**	8.11	-	15-2	8	GD	H.Cecil	S.Cauthen	0-1	
92	4-00111	**LANDOWNER**	8.11	81	8-1	2	GD-FM	J.Gosden	R.Cochrane	3-5	12f
93	12-24	**INFRASONIC**	8.11	111	3-1F	4	SFT	A.Fabre(FR)	Pat Eddery	0-2	
94	1002-31	**SILVER WEDGE**	8.11	90	20-1	8	GD-FM	G.Lewis	M.Hills	1-2	12f
95	1-41	**STELVIO**	8.11	106	7-4F	10	GD-FM	H.Cecil	M.Kinane	1-2	14f
96	-041	**GORDI**	8.11	-	7-1	4	GD-FM	D.Weld(IR)	M.Kinane	1-3	10f
97	11-02	**WINDSOR CASTLE**	8.11	96	9-2(SF)	12	GD-FM	P.Cole	T.Quinn	0-2	
98	-021	**MARIDPOUR**	8.11	92	6-1	5	GD-SFT	Sir M.Stoute	W.Swinburn	1-3	12f
99	-31	**ENDORSMENT**	8.06	85	5-1(SF)	10	GD-FM	H.Cecil	K.Fallon	1-2	12f

FAVOURITES/SECOND FAVOURITES (strike rate and to a £1 stake): **Favs. 27 per cent, +£0.75, S.Favs. 15 per cent, -£1.50.**

AVERAGE WINNING RATING: 94.

TOP TRAINER (wins-runners, strike rate and to a £1 stake): **Henry Cecil (4-16, 20 per cent, +£3.75).**

Introduction

First run in 1838, this race was elevated to Group Three status after spending a period (1986-1990) as a Listed contest. Despite that endorsement, it rarely falls to a top-class stayer.

Ten year analysis

Weight/Rating: The average win rating (94) is particularly low for a Group race, indicating that this is a relatively weak contest.

Form: Six failed to win as two-year-olds, only one running more than twice at that age. Nine had a maximum of three starts during their preparation, seven winning from May, six from 12-14 furlongs. Note that only three ran in a Group race beforehand.

Latest start: All ten had their latest start from May, six winning and two finishing second.

Betting: Favourites show a modest level-stakes profit, second favourites a small loss. The market is an unreliable guide.

Top trainer: Henry Cecil has a tremendous record. The master of Warren Place has sent out four winners from 16 runners since 1990 and should continue to do well.

ROYAL ASCOT, WEDNESDAY JUNE 21
DUKE OF EDINBURGH HANDICAP (0-105) (1m 4f)

YR	FORM	WINNER	AGE-WT	RATING	S.P	DRAW	GOING	TRAINER	JOCKEY	FORM IN YEAR WN-RN	WN DIST.
90	31-1213	**HATEEL**	4 9.00	92	5-1F	17	FM	P.Walwyn	W.Carson	2-4	11,12f
91	0402-42	**RINJA**	4 7.09	77	16-1	16	GD	D.Arbuthnot	J.Lowe	0-2	
92	410-002	**SPINNING**	5 9.03	98	25-1	8	GD-FM	I.Balding	R.Cochrane	0-3	
93	12130-2	**SOURCE OF LIGHT**	4 9.03	94	11-1	4	SFT	R.Charlton	Pat Eddery	0-1	
94	1330-00	**MASTER CHARLIE**	4 9.02	87	10-1	18	GD-FM	I.Balding	L.Dettori	0-2	
95	011-111	**SON OF SHARP SHOT**	5 8.13	90	5-1(SF)	19	GD-FM	J.Dunlop	Pat Eddery	3-3	10,12f
96	000-031	**TYKEVOR**	6 8.01	82	14-1	14	GD-FM	Lady Herries	F.Lynch	1-3	12f
97	212/00-0	**ZARALASKA**	6 8.13	90	8-1	4	GD-FM	L.Cumani	Pat Eddery	0-1	
98	331-0	**GREEK PALACE**	4 9.08	98	9-1(SF)	10	GD-SFT	Sir M.Stoute	W.Swinburn	0-1	
99	23100-1	**BLUEPRINT**	4 9.09	99	4-1F	7	GD-FM	Sir M.Stoute	G.Stevens	1-1	12f

AGE (wins-runners): 3-Y-O: 0-1, 4-Y-O: 6-121, 5-Y-O: 2-44, 6-Y-O+: 2-23.
FAVOURITES/SECOND FAVOURITES (strike rate and to a £1 stake): Favs. 17 per cent, -£2, **S.Favs. 13 per cent, +£1.**
AVERAGE WINNING RATING: 91.

Introduction

Previously known as the Bessborough,with class acts like Hateel, Spinning, Source Of Light, Zaralaska, Greek Palace and Blueprint among its recent winners, this is no ordinary handicap. Do not be surprised if this year's winner develops into a Listed or Group-class performer.

Ten year analysis

Age: While those aged six and above have the best strike rate, four-year-olds boast an impressive six winners since 1990.

Weight/Rating: Rinja and Tykevor are unusual among the recent winners in that they carried less than 8st 13lbs and were rated below 87. Generally, this is best left to those in the top half of the weights.

Draw: High draws are reckoned to be helpful but, as four of the last ten have scored from single-figure stalls, that advantage should not be overestimated.

Form: A recent win is not important – only four scored during their preparation – and it is more pertinent to note that only Hateel ran more than four times earlier in his year. This is a race for unexposed, lightly-raced types who may still be ahead of the Handicapper.

Latest start: All ten had their latest start from 10-12 furlongs during May or June, eight in handicaps.

Betting: Favourites have produced a small level-stakes loss, second favourites a minimal profit. The market is not an outstanding guide.

Top trainer: Sir Michael Stoute has taken this race by the scruff of the neck over the past two seasons, sending out the Group-class pair Greek Dance and Blueprint to land substantial gambles. Keep a close eye on his runners in the future.

ROYAL ASCOT, THURSDAY JUNE 22
RIBBLESDALE STAKES (GROUP 2) THREE-YEAR-OLD FILLIES (1m 4f)

YR	FORM	WINNER	WT	RATING	S.P.	DRAW	GOING	TRAINER	JOCKEY	FORM IN YEAR WN-RN	WN DIST.
90	4-1	**HELLENIC**	8.08	-	6-1	2	GD-SFT	Sir M.Stoute	W.Swinburn	1-1	10f
91	10-0	**THIRD WATCH**	8.08	-	20-1	7	GD	J.Dunlop	J.Reid	0-1	
92	02-2232	**ARMARAMA**	8.08	-	5-2F	7	GD-FM	C.Brittain	M.Roberts	0-4	
93	011-4	**THAWAKIB**	8.08	108	5-2F	4	SFT	J.Dunlop	W.Carson	0-1	
94	0-1	**BOLAS**	8.08	-	3-1F	4	GD-FM	B.Hills	Pat Eddery	1-1	11f
95	31-30	**PHANTOM GOLD**	8.08	100	5-1(SF)	1	GD-FM	Ld Huntingdon	L.Dettori	0-2	
96	03-112	**TULIPA**	8.08	-	15-2	10	GD-FM	A.Fabre(FR)	S.Guillot	2-3	10f
97	122-014	**YASHMAK**	8.08	114	7-2(SF)	2	GD	H.Cecil	K.Fallon	1-3	10f
98	11-12	**BAHR**	8.08	114	13-8F	6	GD-SFT	S.Bin Suroor	L.Dettori	1-2	10f
99	11-01	**FAIRY QUEEN**	8.08	105	8-1	3	GD-FM	S.Bin Suroor	L.Dettori	1-2	8.5f

FAVOURITES/SECOND FAVOURITES (strike rate and to a £1 stake): **Favs. 40 per cent, +£3.62,** S.Favs. 15 per cent, -£2.50.
AVERAGE WINNING RATING: 105

Introduction

Used as a consolation prize for those who were not ready to run in the Oaks, this rarely falls to an outstanding performer and is often won by a late-developing stayer.

Ten year analysis

Form: Six won as two-year-olds, although it is more interesting to note that none ran more than three times at that age.
Five won and two finished placed in a Group or Listed event earlier in their three-year-old campaign, indicating that your selection should be proven at a decent level of competition.

Latest start: Nine ran in a Group or Listed race on their latest start, two winning and five making the frame. Avoid any taking a big step-up in class.

Betting: Favourites boast a useful 40 per cent strike rate and level-stakes profit. While shocks can occur – witness Third Watch (20-1) in 1991 – the market is a fair guide.

Top trainer: Saeed Bin Suroor has sent out the last two winners – Bahr and Fairy Queen – while Sir Michael Stoute has a consistent record. Although responsible for just one winner, Sir Michael has saddled six placed fillies since 1990, and his entrants have every chance of making the frame.

ROYAL ASCOT, THURSDAY JUNE 22
NORFOLK STAKES (GROUP 3) TWO-YEAR-OLDS (5f)

									FORM IN YEAR	
YR	FORM	WINNER	WT	S.P.	DRAW	GOING	TRAINER	JOCKEY	WN-RN	WN DIST.
90	3	**LINE ENGAGED**	8.13	14-1	10	GD-SFT	D.Elsworth	S.Cauthen	0-1	
91	11*	**MAGIC RING**	8.13	7-4F	7	GD	P.Cole	A.Munro	1-2	5f
92	11	**NICHE**	8.08	9-1	5	GD-FM	R.Hannon	L.Piggott	2-2	5f
93	1	**TURTLE ISLAND**	8.13	3-1(SF)	1	SFT	P.Chapple-Hyam	J.Reid	1-1	5f
94	11	**MIND GAMES**	8.13	5-2(SF)	2	GD-FM	J.Berry	J.Carroll	2-2	5f
95	14	**LUCKY LIONEL**	8.12	11-1	1	GD-FM	R.Hannon	L.Dettori	1-2	5f
96	1	**TIPSY CREEK**	8.12	7-2F	11	GD-FM	B.Hanbury	W.Ryan	1-1	5f
97	3001	**TIPPITT BOY**	8.12	33-1	2	GD	K.McAuliffe	J.Reid	1-4	6f
98	11	**ROSSELLI**	8.12	10-1	1	GD-SFT	J.Berry	J.Carroll	2-2	5f
99	1	**WARM HEART**	8.12	7-2(SF)	11	GD-FM	J.Gosden	L.Dettori	1-1	5f

* Disqualified

FAVOURITES/SECOND FAVOURITES (strike rate and to a £1 stake): Favs. 25 per cent, -£4.75, **S.Favs. 27 per cent, +£1.**

RACE RECORD: With Niche, Turtle Island and Mind Games among its recent winners, this must be regarded as a warm contest.

Introduction

This has been won by a mixed bag of horses. Niche, Turtle Island and Mind Games developed into high-class performers, while Line Engaged, Magic Ring and Rosselli were ultimately disappointing.

Ten Year analysis

Form: Line Engaged is the only maiden to have won this in the past decade. The remainder scored beforehand, only one beyond five furlongs. Avoid over-exposed youngsters – nine had a maximum of two previous starts.

Latest start: All ten had their latest outing from May, eight winning (one was disqualified). This is a race for last-start scorers.

Betting: Only two favourites have scored since 1990, while there have been long-priced winners like Line Engaged (14/1), Lucky Lionel (11/1) and Tippitt Boy (33/1) during the same period. Do not rely on the market as a guide.

Top trainer: Richard Hannon is a dab hand with sharp juveniles. He has saddled two winners, two seconds and two thirds in this contest over the past decade and is definitely number one in our chart.

ROYAL ASCOT, THURSDAY JUNE 22
GOLD CUP (GROUP 1) (2m 4f)

YR	FORM	WINNER	AGE-WT	RATING	S.P.	DRAW	GOING	TRAINER	JOCKEY	FORM IN YEAR WN-RN	WN DIST.
90	2111-21	**ASHAL**	4 9.00	-	14-1	5	GD-SFT	H.T.Jones	R.Hills	1-2	16f
91	301-203	**INDIAN QUEEN**	6 8.13	110	25-1	9	GD	Ld Huntingdon	W.Swinburn	0-3	
92	1120-11	**DRUM TAPS**	6 9.02	113	7-4F	3	GD-FM	Ld Huntingdon	L.Dettori	2-2	15,16f
93	11232-1	**DRUM TAPS**	7 9.02	117	13-2	6	SFT	Ld Huntingdon	L.Dettori	1-1	15f
94	0300-30	**ARCADIAN HEIGHTS**	6 9.02	101	20-1	5	GD-FM	G.Wragg	M.Hills	0-2	
95	310-141	**DOUBLE TRIGGER**	4 9.00	1[illegible]	9-4(SF)	6	GD-FM	M.Johnston	J.Weaver	2-3	16f
96	14201-1	**CLASSIC CLICHE**	4 9.00	120	3-1(SF)	7	GD-FM	S.Bin Suroor	M.Kinane	1-1	14f
97	121-412	**CELERIC**	5 9.02	117	11-2(SF)	2	GD	D.Morley	Pat Eddery	1-3	14f
98	21-13	**KAYF TARA**	4 9.00	111	11-1	1	SFT	S.Bin Suroor	L.Dettori	1-2	12f
99	11341-1	**ENZELI**	4 9.00	1[illegible]7	20-1	16	GD-FM	J.Oxx(IR)	J.Murtagh	1-1	14f

AGE (wins-runners): 4-Y-O: 5-44, 5-Y-O: 1-32, 6-Y-O+: 4-32.

FAVOURITES/SECOND FAVOURITES (strike rate and to a £1 stake): Favs. 10 per cent, -£7.25, **S.Favs. 27 per cent, +£2.75.**

AVERAGE WINNING RATING: 113.

Introduction

Seen as an anachronism in the eighties, the Gold Cup has shot back into vogue through the exploits of high-profile stayers like Drum Taps, Double Trigger, Classic Cliché and Kayf Tara.

Ten year analysis

Age: Five-year-olds are the weak link. This is usually best left to four-year-olds or horses aged six and above.

Weight/Rating: The average win rating of 113 is unexceptional for a Group One event. Horses rated 101 (Arcadian Heights) and 107 (Enzeli) have scored recently, and your selection need not possess the mark of a superstar.

Form: Eight won over at least 14 furlongs during their preparation, six landing a Group event.
Avoid those who have been kept busy – none appeared more than three times beforehand – and remember that only two ran outside Group or Listed company. This is not a race for horses taking a huge step-up in class.

Latest start: Nine ran in a Group race during May last time, five winning and three making the frame.

Best trial: Sandown's Henry II Stakes (run on May 29) is easily the best trial. Five of the last ten ran there, Drum Taps and Double Trigger winning, Celeric and Kayf Tara making the frame, while Arcadian Heights finished unplaced.

Betting: Drum Taps (1992) is the last winning favourite and second favourites have a superior record. That said, shocks are commonplace – witness Ashal (14/1), Indian Queen (25/1), Arcadian Heights (20/1) and Enzeli (20/1) – and it could pay to look for some value.

Top trainer: This could become a benefit for Saeed Bin Suroor and the Godolphin team. They have saddled two winners and two placed horses over the past four seasons.

ROYAL ASCOT, THURSDAY JUNE 22
CORK AND ORRERY STAKES (GROUP 2) (6f)

YR	FORM	WINNER	AGE-WT	RATING	S.P.	DRAW	GOING	TRAINER	JOCKEY	FORM IN YEAR WN-RN	WN DIST.
90	24122-2	**GREAT COMMOTION**	4 9.00	115	5-1(SF)	8	GD-SFT	A.Scott	Pat Eddery	0-1	
91	12210-1	**POLISH PATRIOT**	3 8.02	105	5-1JF	2	GD	G.Harwood	R.Cochrane	1-1	6f

92	014-101	**SHALFORD**	4 9.04	120	3-1F	16	GD-FM	R.Hannon	M.Roberts	2-3	6,7f
93	-11	**COLLEGE CHAPEL**	3 8.10	-	7-2F	3	SFT	M.V.O'Brien(IR)	L.Piggott	2-2	6,7f
94	3112-01	**OWINGTON**	3 8.10	117	4-1F	2	GD-FM	G.Wragg	M.Hills	1-2	6f
95	21112-2	**SO FACTUAL**	5 8.13	114	9-2(SF)	9	GD-FM	S.Bin Suroor	L.Dettori	0-1	
96	00-1221	**ATRAF**	3 8.06	109	12-1	2	GD-FM	D.Morley	W.Carson	2-4	6f
97	0010-11	**ROYAL APPLAUSE**	4 9.03	117	11-2F	16	GD	B.Hills	M.Hills	2-2	6f
98	1233-44	**TOMBA**	4 9.00	116	4-1(SF)	13	SFT	B.Meehan	M.Tebbutt	0-2	
99	0201-10	**BOLD EDGE**	4 9.00	112	16-1	16	GD-FM	R.Hannon	D.O'Neill	1-2	6f

AGE (wins-runners): 3-Y-O: 4-72, 4-Y-O: 5-54, 5-Y-O: 1-23 6-Y-O+: 0-19.

FAVOURITES/SECOND FAVOURITES (strike rate and to a £1 stake): **Favs. 45 per cent, +£15**, S.Favs. 25 per cent, +-£4.50.

AVERAGE WINNING RATING: 114.

Introduction

With an average field of 16 runners, this is always fiercely competitive. The recent winners include Polish Patriot, Owington, Royal Applause and Tomba, who all went on to land a Group One event. Their successor is worth noting in races like the July Cup and Haydock Park Sprint Cup.

Ten year analysis

Age: Three and four-year-olds have dominated this event over the past decade. Look beyond them at your peril.

Weight/Rating: Four of the last ten carried the penalty for winning a Group race. Extra poundage is not insurmountable.

Draw: Those drawn high (13-16) have won the last three runnings. However, as four others have come from stalls two or three, the draw does not seem overly important.

Form: Seven won during their preparation, six in Group or Listed events around six furlongs. That indicates that this is a race for proven horses, a point underlined by the fact that only one ran in a handicap beforehand.

Latest start: Nine ran in a six-furlong Group or Listed event from May on their latest start, five winning and three making the frame.

Best trial: The Duke Of York Stakes has been an excellent pointer. Six of the last ten ran in that Group Three contest, Shalford, Owington and Royal Applause winning, Great Commotion and So Factual finishing second and Bold Edge unplaced.

Betting: While there have been a couple of blips – Atraf (12/1) and Bold Edge (16/1) –favourites boast an excellent 45 per cent strike rate and a mouthwatering 15 point level-stakes profit.

Top trainer: This is another race where Richard Hannon leads the field. The East Everleigh handler has saddled two winners and two placed horses since 1990.

ROYAL ASCOT, THURSDAYJUNE 22
CHESHAM STAKES (LISTED) TWO-YEAR-OLDS (7f)

YR	FORM	WINNER	WT	S.P.	DRAW	GOING	TRAINER	JOCKEY	FORM IN YEAR WN-RN	WN DIST.
90	1	**CHICARICA**	8.07	10-11F	7	GD-SFT	J.Gosden	Pat Eddery	1-1	6f
91	11	**FAIR COP**	8.12	7-2JF	4	GD	P.Cole	A.Munro	2-2	6f
92	1	**HUMAM**	8.12	2-1F	2	GD-FM	H.T.Jones	R.Hills	1-1	6f
93	1	**STATE PERFORMER**	9.00	8-13F	6	SFT	P.Chapple-Hyam	J.Reid	1-1	6f
94	3	**MONTJOY**	8.12	5-1(SF)	3	GD-FM	P.Cole	T.Quinn	0-1	
95	1202	**WORLD PREMIER**	9.02	6-1	5	GD-FM	C.Brittain	B.Doyle	1-4	5f
96		**SHAMIKH**	8.12	8-1	4	GD-FM	S.Bin Suroor	R.Hills	0-0	
97	41	**CENTRAL PARK**	9.00	7-1	6	GD	P.Cole	L.Dettori	1-2	6f
98	2	**RHAPSODIST**	8.12	6-1	8	SFT	J.Gosden	L.Dettori	0-1	
99	1	**BACH**	8.12	5-2(SF)	5	GD-FM	A.O'Brien	M.Kinane	1-1	7f

* Run over six furlongs prior to 1996.

FAVOURITES/SECOND FAVOURITES (strike rate and to a £1 stake): **Favs. 36 per cent, +£0.03,** S.Favs. 15 per cent, -£3.50.
TOP TRAINER (wins-runners, strike rate and to a £1 stake): **Paul Cole (3-9, 33 per cent, +£9.50).**

Introduction

Run over six furlongs up until 1995, this race is restricted to juveniles sired by a horse that won over a mile and a quarter or beyond.
While several recent winners have been a shade disappointing, this can throw up decent horses, witness the fact that Central Park beat Cape Verdi back in 1997.

Ten year analysis

Form: Eight had a one or two-start preparation, seven winning, six from May. Note that World Premier is the only winner who ran before May or below six furlongs.

Latest start: Six won from May on their latest start, five scoring in maiden company.

Betting: Favourites were dominant in the early nineties, but none have won since 1993. All the winners in the interim started between 5/2 and 7/1, hinting that this is best left to those just beyond the market leader.

Top trainer: Paul Cole has done particularly well in the Chesham Stakes over the past decade, saddling three winners (Fair Cop, Montjoy and Central Park) four placed horses and two who finished out of the money. Expect a bold show from anything he runs.

ROYAL ASCOT, THURSDAY JUNE 22
KING GEORGE V HANDICAP (0-105) THREE-YEAR-OLDS (1m 4f)

YR	FORM	WINNER	WT	RATING	S.P.	DRAW	GOING	TRAINER	JOCKEY	FORM IN YEAR WN-RN	WN DIST.
90	201-041	**LIFT AND LOAD**	9.01	91	20-1	15	GD-SFT	R.Hannon	B.Rouse	1-3	10f
91	0-01	**TORCHON**	8.07	90	8-1	12	GD	G.Wragg	G.Carter	1-2	10f
92	-12	**SOURCE OF LIGHT**	8.10	87	12-1	17	GD-FM	R.Charlton	Pat Eddery	1-2	10f
93	0-0041	**LEARMONT**	8.08	81	14-1	2	SFT	J.Gosden	J.Carroll	1-4	10f
94	010-103	**MIDNIGHT LEGEND**	8.07	82	9-1	20	GD-FM	L.Cumani	J.Weaver	1-3	8f
95	2203-14	**DIAGHILEF**	9.07	99	40-1	15	GD-FM	M.Johnston	D.Holland	1-2	10f
96	4-131	**SAMRAAN**	9.03	94	14-1	17	GD-FM	J.Dunlop	T.Quinn	2-3	10,12f
97	4-31	**HERITAGE**	8.06	82	15-2(SF)	14	GD	J.Gosden	L.Dettori	1-2	10.5f
98	03-121	**DOUBLE CLASSIC**	8.12	94	4-1F	7	SFT	Sir M.Stoute	J.Reid	2-3	8,12f
99	0-422	**ELMUTABAKI**	8.12	90	9-1	7	GD-FM	B.Hills	R.Hills	0-3	

FAVOURITES/SECOND FAVOURITES (strike rate and to a £1 stake): Favs. 7 per cent, -£9, **S.Favs. 7 per cent, -£5.50.**
AVERAGE WINNING RATING: 89.

Introduction

Torchon, Source Of Light, Midnight Legend, Samraan and Elmutabaki went on to make the grade in Listed or Group races after winning here. This is no ordinary handicap and the winner must be followed.

Ten year analysis

Weight/Rating: None of the last ten carried less than 8st 6lbs or were rated below 81. This is not a race for those in the bottom half of the weights.

Draw: Only Learmont (stall two) came from a very low draw. Those drawn high hold a slight tactical advantage.

Form: This is a race for late-developing types who have given the Handicapper precious little chance to assess them accurately. Only two of the last ten won as two-year-olds, the majority being lightly-raced at that age (five had just one start).

Nine won earlier in their year, eight over 10-12 furlongs from May. Only Learmont ran more than three times during his preparation.

Latest start: Six won from 10-12 furlongs on their latest start, three landing handicaps and three others picking-up a maiden. The remaining quartet all made the frame, indicating that those who come here on the back of a disappointment should be avoided.

Betting: Favourites and second favourites have dismal records, producing just one winner apiece since 1990. Look beyond the market leaders when making your selection.

Top trainer: There are no outstanding records, John Gosden's two winners and one placed horse being the best clue on offer.

ROYAL ASCOT, FRIDAY JUNE 23
KING EDWARD VII STAKES THREE-YEAR-OLDS (1m 4f)

YR FORM	WINNER	WT	RATING	S.P.	DRAW	GOING	TRAINER	JOCKEY	FORM IN YEAR WN-RN	WN DIST.
90 -101	**PRIVATE TENDER**	8.08	-	11-4F	2	GD-FM	H.Cecil	S.Cauthen	2-3	10,12f
91 0-12	**SADDLERS' HALL**	8.08	-	7-1	10	GD	Sir M.Stoute	L.Piggott	1-2	10f
92 103-144	**BEYTON**	8.08	-	12-1	6	GD-FM	R.Hannon	M.Kinane	1-3	11f
93 11-1212	**BENEFICIAL**	8.08	111	11-4F	5	SFT	G.Wragg	M.Hills	2-4	9,10f
94 -31U	**FOYER**	8.08	-	7-2(SF)	1	GD-FM	Sir M.Stoute	M.Kinane	1-3	10f
95 330-111	**PENTIRE**	8.08	113	4-1(SF)	4	FM	G.Wragg	M.Hills	3-3	10f
96 -000	**AMFORTAS**	8.08	86	66-1	6	GD-FM	C.Brittain	B.Doyle	0-3	
97 0-14	**KINGFISHER MILL**	8.08	112	9-4F	2	SFT	J.Cecil	Pat Eddery	1-2	10f
98 -11	**ROYAL ANTHEM**	8.08	-	9-4F	1	GD-SFT	H.Cecil	K.Fallon	2-2	10f
99 21-1	**MUTAFAWEQ**	8.08	-	4-1F	9	GD-FM	S.Bin Suroor	L.Dettori	1-1	10f

FAVOURITES/SECOND FAVOURITES (strike rate and to a £1 stake): **Favs. 45 per cent, +£8, S.Favs. 20 per cent, -£0.50.**
AVERAGE WINNING RATING: 105.

Introduction

Known as Royal Ascot's Derby, this race cannot compare with the Epsom showpiece. That said, it has been won by some cracking horses – Pentire, Royal Anthem and Mutafaweq for example – and the winner should be followed.

Weight/Rating: Few recent winners had an official rating and this is best left to unexposed, improving individuals.

Form: Only four of the last ten scored as two-year-olds, underlining that this is a race for slow-maturing types.
Nine won from 10-12 furlongs earlier in their year, none running more than four times.
Another vital factor is that only one – Foyer – ran in a Classic during his preparation. Derby also-rans often figure prominently in the betting but, statistically, they face an uphill struggle.

Latest start: Four won a ten-furlong minor or Listed event on their latest start, only Amfortas failing to make the frame.

Betting: Favourites boast an excellent 45 per cent strike rate and a healthy eight-point level-stakes profit. That tally includes the last three winners and the market is a fair guide.

Top trainers: Sir Michael Stoute has saddled two winners and two placed horses since 1990 and has the best record available. Henry Cecil – two winners and one placed – is another trainer to note.

ROYAL ASCOT, FRIDAY JUNE 23
HARDWICKE STAKES (GROUP 2) (1m 4f)

YR	FORM IN YEAR FORM	WINNER	AGE-WT	RATING	S.P.	DRAW	GOING	TRAINER	JOCKEY	WN-RN	WN DIST.
90	12110-4	**ASSATIS**	5 9.00	121	50-1	6	GD-SFT	G.Harwood	Pat Eddery	0-1	
*91	1/21-113	**ROCK HOPPER**	4 8.12	122	5-6F	2	GD	M.Stoute	Pat Eddery	2-3	12f
92	320-012	**ROCK HOPPER**	5 8.12	122	8-15F	2	GD-FM	M.Stoute	Pat Eddery	1-3	14f
93	2012-33	**JEUNE**	4 8.09	112	7-2(SF)	4	SFT	G.Wragg	R.Cochrane	0-2	
94	2200-33	**BOBZAO**	5 8.09	113	11-1	8	GD-FM	T.Mills	J.Reid	0-2	
95	000-331	**BEAUCHAMP HERO**	5 8.09	100	11-2	1	FM	J.Dunlop	J.Reid	1-3	12f
96	0443-21	**OSCAR SCHINDLER**	4 8.09	117	7-4F	8	GD-FM	K.Prendergast(IR)	M.Kinane	1-2	13f
97	12311-2	**PREDAPPIO**	4 8.12	-	6-1(SF)	7	GD	S.Bin Suroor	G.Stevens	0-1	
98	3102-10	**POSIDONAS**	6 8.09	117	15-2	7	GD-SFT	P.Cole	Pat Eddery	1-2	12f
99	0040-10	**FRUITS OF LOVE**	4 8.12	120	12-1	9	GD-FM	M.Johnston	O.Peslier	1-2	12f

*TOPANOORA 4 8.09, 8-1, J.Bolger(IR), C.Roche finished first but was disqualified for interference and placed second.

AGE (wins-runners): 4-Y-O: 5-55, **5-Y-O: 4-15,** 6-Y-O+: 1-7.

FAVOURITES/SECOND FAVOURITES (strike rate and to a £1 stake): Favs. 30 per cent, -£3.89, **S.Favs. 14 per cent, -£2.50.**

AVERAGE WINNING RATING: 116.

Introduction

This is a hot race, but rarely falls to an outstanding middle-distance horse. The likes of Assatis, Rock Hopper, Jeune, Bobzao and Beauchamp Hero were found out when tried against Group One horses and a similar fate may befall their successor.

Ten year analysis

Weight/Rating: Beauchamp Hero (rated 100) drags the average winning mark down, although 116 is respectable. Stick with proven performers.

Form: A recent win is not important and it is more useful to note that none ran more than three times beforehand. This is a race for fresh horses.

Latest start: Eight ran in a Group race on their latest start, one winning and five making the frame. Avoid those taking a big step-up in class.

Best trials: The Jockey Club Stakes (run at Newmarket on May 5) has been the most reliable trial. Five ran in that contest, Rock Hopper winning in 1991, Assatis, Jeune and Bobzao making the frame, while Rock Hopper was unplaced as a five-year-old in 1992. Epsom's Coronation Cup is another sound trial. Four ran there, two making the frame and two finishing unplaced.

Betting: While favourites and second favourites have a weak record, this has produced several shock results – Assatis (50/1), Bobzao (11/1) and Fruits Of Love (12/1). Look for some value.

Top trainer: Sir Michael Stoute has the best record, producing two winners and three placed horses over the last decade.

ROYAL ASCOT, FRIDAY JUNE 23
WOKINGHAM HANDICAP (0-110) (6f)

YR	FORM	WINNER	AGE-WT	RATING	S.P.	DRAW	GOING	TRAINER	JOCKEY	FORM IN YEAR WN-RN	WN DIST.
90	0-04341	**KNIGHT OF MERCY**	4 8.06	92	16-1	17	GD-SFT	R.Hannon	Pat Eddery	1-5	7f
91	210-001	**AMIGO MENOR**	5 8.07	91	14-1	4	GD	D.Murray-Smith	C.Rutter	1-3	6f
92	0-00433	**RED ROSEIN**	6 8.01	80	33-1	29	GD-FM	Capt.J.Wilson	G.Carter	0-5	
93	0320-03	**NAGIDA**	4 8.07	84	11-1	4	SFT	J.Toller	J.Weaver	0-2	

94	00032-0	**VENTURE CAPITALIST**	5 8.12	91	20-1	30	GD-FM	R.Hannon	J.Reid	0-1	
95	30231-0	**ASTRAC**	4 8.07	89	14-1	16	FM	R.Akehurst	S.Sanders	0-1	
96	402-440	**EMERGING MARKET**	4 8.13	95	33-1	7	GD-FM	J.Dunlop	K.Darley	0-3	
97	100-223	**SELHURSTPARK FLYER**	6 8.09	94	25-1	5	GD-SFT	J.Berry	P.Roberts	0-3	
98	00-0401	**SELHURSTPARK FLYER**	7 9.07	100	16-1	20	GD-SFT	J.Berry	C.Lowther	1-4	6f
99	00-0102	**DEEP SPACE**	4 8.07	88	14-1	3	GD-FM	E.Dunlop	G.Carter	1-4	7f

AGE (wins-runners): 3-Y-O: 0-24, **4-Y-O: 5-108**, 5-Y-O: 2-69, 6-Y-O+: 3-93.
FAVOURITES/SECOND FAVOURITES (strike rate and to a £1 stake): **Favs. 0 per cent, -£10**, S.Favs. 0 per cent, -£15.

AVERAGE WINNING RATING: 90.

Introduction

Fiercely competitive, this race traditionally encourages a lively ante-post market. However, as no first favourite has scored since Bel Byou in 1987, the bookmakers have definitely had the better of the argument.

Ten year analysis

Age: Three-year-olds have a dismal record – it is 13 years since one scored – and four-year-olds have the best strike rate.

Weight/Rating: Nine carried between 8st 1lb and 8st 13lbs – it should pay to concentrate on those sited in this section of the weights. Ratings-wise, our ten-year average of 90 is a fair guide to the level of ability required to score.

Draw: The Ascot draw is always contentious and, as high and low numbers have shared the spoils over the past decade, it is probably best to remain open-minded.

Form: None of the last ten ran more than five times during their preparation. Lightly-raced types who could still be ahead of the Handicapper are preferred. Eight managed to make the frame from May, and your selection should have shown some tangible signs of form.

Latest start: Eight had their latest start in a handicap from May, two winning and four making the frame.

Betting: This is a terrible race for market leaders. No first or second favourite has scored during the period under study, while outsiders have struck at 20/1, 25/1 and 33/1 (two).

Top trainer: Richard Hannon usually has a decent sprint handicapper among his team, and has sent out two winners and four placed horses over the past ten seasons.

ROYAL ASCOT, FRIDAY JUNE 23
KING'S STAND STAKES (GROUP 2) (5f)

YR	FORM	WINNER	AGE-WT	RATING	S.P.	DRAW	GOING	TRAINER	JOCKEY	FORM IN YEAR WN-RN	WN DIST.
90	12-0121	**DAYJUR**	3 8.10	-	11-2	9	GD-SFT	W.Hern	W.Carson	2-4	5,6f
91	110-211	**ELBIO**	4 9.03	-	13-8F	8	GD	P.Makin	S.Cauthen	2-3	5f
92	141221-	**SHEIKH ALBADOU**	4 9.03	125	7-2JF	1	GD-FM	A.Scott	W.Swinburn	0-0	
93	404130-	**ELBIO**	6 9.03	117	12-1	1	SFT	P.Makin	W.Swinburn	0-0	
94	1131-11	**LOCHSONG**	6 9.00	123	30-100F	4	GD-FM	I.Balding	L.Dettori	2-2	5f
95	1200-03	**PICCOLO**	4 9.06	113	20-1	7	FM	M.Channon	R.Hughes	0-2	
96	011-	**PIVOTAL**	3 8.10	104	13-2	7	GD-FM	Sir. M.Prescott	G.Duffield	0-0	
97	201-004	**DON'T WORRY ME**	5 8.13	-	33-1	4	GD-SFT	G.Henrot(FR)	O.Peslier	0-3	
98	000-011	**BOLSHOI**	6 9.02	108	10-1	20	GD-SFT	J.Berry	C.Lowther	2-3	5f
99	12-2310	**MITCHAM**	3 8.10	102	20-1	3	GD-FM	T.Mills	T.Quinn	1-4	6f

AGE (wins-runners): 3-Y-O: 3-50, 4-Y-O: 3-39, 5-Y-O: 1-20, **6-Y-O+: 3-23.**

FAVOURITES/SECOND FAVOURITES (strike rate and to a £1 stake): **Favs. 23 per cent, -£4.55,** S.Favs. 0 per cent, -£10.

AVERAGE WINNING RATING: 113.

Introduction

While outstanding sprinters like Dayjur, Sheikh Albadou and Lochsong figure on the roll of honour, this has fallen to some sub-standard horses. Three of the last four had the rating of a decent handicapper when scoring, and this is definitely a race where the established stars can be taken on.

Ten year analysis

Age: While those aged six and above have the best strike rate, there is no real age bias.

Weight/Rating: With such as Pivotal (104), Bolshoi (108) and Mitcham (102) scoring recently, those rated below our average winning mark (113) have every chance.

Form: Three seasonal debutants have scored since 1990. Do not discount those who come here without the benefit of a preparatory race.
Five of the seven who had a previous outing managed to score. If your selection has run, he should have won.

Latest start: Six ran in a five or six-furlong Group race during May on their latest start, four winning and two making the frame.

Best trial: The Temple Stakes, run on May 29 at Sandown, has been the best guide. Dayjur, Elbio (in 1991), Lochsong and Bolshoi won that contest immediately before scoring here.

Betting: Favourites and second favourites have produced poor results to a level stakes wager over the past decade.
With winners returning at 12/1, 20/1 (twice) and 33/1, this is a fair race for outsiders.

ROYAL ASCOT, FRIDAY JUNE 23
WINDSOR CASTLE STAKES TWO-YEAR-OLDS (5f)

YR	FORM	WINNER	WT	S.P.	DRAW	GOING	TRAINER	JOCKEY	FORM IN YEAR WN-RN	WN DIST.
90	11	GIPSY FIDDLER	9.06	7-2(SF)	8	GD-SFT	J.J.O'Neill	Pat Eddery	2-2	5f
91		ISDAR	8.13	8-1	7	GD	H.T.Jones	R.Hills	0-0	
92	3	SATANK	8.13	7-1	7	GD-FM	J.W.Watts	Pat Eddery	0-1	
93	1	GREAT DEEDS	8.06	10-1	2	SFT	M.Channon	T.Quinn	1-1	6f
94	2	BRAVE MUSIC	8.11	9-1	13	GD-FM	P.Cole	T.Quinn	0-1	
95		KUANTAN	8.11	11-1	7	FM	P.Cole	T.Quinn	0-0	
96		DAZZLE	8.05	7-2F	11	GD-FM	M.Stoute	K.Fallon	0-0	
97	2	ASFURAH	8.06	7-1(SF)	8	SFT	S.Bin Suroor	R.Hills	0-1	
98	11	FLANDERS	8.10	15-8F	14	GD-SFT	T.D.Easterby	L.Charnock	2-2	5f
99	02	KALINDI	8.06	14-1	12	GD-FM	M.Channon	T.Quinn	0-2	

FAVOURITES/SECOND FAVOURITES (strike rate and to a £1 stake): Favs. 20 per cent, -£2.63. **S.Favs. 17 per cent, +£0.50.**

Introduction

This is the weakest of Royal Ascot's juvenile events. Dazzle and Flanders aside, the recent winners are a nondescript bunch.

Ten year analysis

Weight/Rating: With cumulative penalties accrued for wins in Class A, B, C and D races, it is no surprise that maidens have a decent record. Pay close attention to unpenalised runners.

Form: Seven maidens have won in the past decade, three being well touted newcomers. Avoid those who are penalised for a previous success.
The seven with previous experienced all made the frame from May, only one running beyond six furlongs. None had more than two outings beforehand.

Latest start: Six ran during June on their latest start, none finishing unplaced.

Betting: This is not a particularly good race for followers of the market, although second favourites have produced a minuscule level-stakes profit since 1990.

Top trainer: Mick Channon does well with nippy youngsters and has saddled two winners and a placed horse during the last decade.

ROYAL ASCOT, FRIDAY JUNE 23
QUEEN ALEXANDRA STAKES (2m 6f)

YR	FORM	WINNER	AGE-WT	RATING	S.P.	DRAW	GOING	TRAINER	JOCKEY	FORM IN YEAR WN-RN	WN DIST.
90	1131-01	**REGAL REFORM**	7 9.04	-	5-1(SF)	5	GD-SFT	G.M.Moore	D.McKeown	1-2	16f
91	02-1332	**EASY TO PLEASE**	4 8.11	92	8-1	3	GD	J.Bolger(IR)	C.Roche	1-4	12f
92	1123-31	**ROMANY RYE**	4 9.02	100	3-1(SF)	8	GD-FM	G.Wragg	W.Swinburn	1-2	16f
93	21321	**RISZARD**	4 8.12	-	9-2	6	SFT	J.Bolger(IR)	C.Roche	2-5	12,14f
94	322-210	**CUFF LINK**	4 9.00	93	6-1	6	GD-FM	W.Hern	Pat Eddery	1-3	14f
95	0204-10	**CUFF LINK**	5 9.04	108	EV F	7	FM	W.Hern	Paul Eddery	1-2	14f
96	30140-4	**ADMIRAL'S WELL**	6 9.03	108	100-30F	1	GD-FM	R.Akehurst	T.Quinn	0-1	
97	4113-14	**CANON CAN**	4 9.01	97	8-1	10	SFT	H.Cecil	K.Fallon	1-2	16f
98	0-34200	**DOVEDON STAR**	4 8.07	82	12-1	10	GD-SFT	A.Kelleway	L.Dettori	0-5	
99	2113-03	**SAN SEBASTIAN**	5 9.00	103	4-1(SF)	5	GD-FM	M.Grassick(IR)	M.Kinane	0-2	

AGE (wins-runners): **4-Y-O: 6-30,** 5-Y-O: 2-22, 6-Y-O+: 2-50.
FAVOURITES/SECOND FAVOURITES (strike rate and to a £1 stake): Favs. 18 per cent, -£6.67, **S.Favs. 33 per cent, -£0.67.**
AVERAGE WINNING RATING: 98.

Introduction

This race usually attracts a hotch-potch of entrants, ranging from hurdlers and chasers to those who fall just short of Group class.

Ten year analysis

Age: Four-year-olds have won six of the last ten runnings and boast easily the best strike rate.

Weight/Rating: None of the recent winners had the mark of a top-class horse, although only one was rated below 92.

Form: While seven scored beforehand – six over at least 14 furlongs - the most interesting form factor is that five won and three made the frame in a non-handicap during their preparation.

Latest start: None ran below 14 furlongs on their latest start. Any taking a huge step-up in trip should be ignored.

Betting: Blind support of favourites and second favourites has yielded a level-stakes loss since 1990. Do not be afraid to look beyond the obvious.

Top trainers: Henry Cecil likes to saddle a fancied runner, and has sent out a winner and four placed horses over the past decade. However, it is equally interesting to note that Irish-trained horses have scored three times during the same period.

NEWCASTLE, SATURDAY JULY 31
NORTHUMBERLAND PLATE HANDICAP (2m)

YR	FORM	WINNER	AGE-WT	RATING	S.P.	DRAW	GOING	TRAINER	JOCKEY	FORM IN YEAR WN-RN	WN DIST.
90	0121-01	**AL MAHEB**	4 8.11	99	9-2(SF)	7	GD-FM	A.Stewart	W.Carson	1-2	13f
91	22000-2	**TAMARPOUR**	4 7.07	69	10-1	9	GD-FM	M.Pipe	E.Johnson	0-1	
92	110-012	**WITNESS BOX**	5 9.09	95	6-1(SF)	9	GD-FM	J.Gosden	G.Duffield	1-3	16f
93	00-0011	**HIGHFLYING**	7 7.11	73	7-1	20	GD-FM	G.Moore	J.Fanning	2-4	12f
94	321-000	**QUICK RANSOM**	6 8.08	95	25-1	4	FM	M.Johnston	J.Weaver	0-3	
95	1210-10	**BOLD GAIT**	4 9.10	105	12-1	5	FM	J.Fanshawe	D.Harrison	1-2	16f
96	213-012	**CELERIC**	4 9.04	96	2-1F	7	FM	D.Morley	W.Carson	1-3	14f
97	11-021	**WINDSOR CASTLE**	3 8.10	104	10-1	20	HVY	P.Cole	T.Quinn	1-3	16f
98	000-340	**CYRIAN**	4 7.13	85	12-1	2	SFT	P.Cole	T.Sprake	0-3	
99	1-13112	**FAR CRY**	4 8.10	89	9-2JF	6	GD-FM	M.Pipe	K.Darley	3-5	16f

AGE (wins-runners): 3-Y-O: 1-6, 4-Y-O: 6-84, 5-Y-O: 1-35, 6-Y-O+: 2-40.
FAVOURITES/SECOND FAVOURITES (strike rate and to a £1 stake): Favs. 17 per cent, -£3.50, S.Favs. 18 per cent, +£1.50.
AVERAGE WINNING RATING: 91.

Introduction

Al Maheb, Witness Box, Quick Ransom, Celeric and Far Cry made the grade in Group races after winning this prestigious contest. Your selection should have sufficient potential to reach that level of competition.

Ten year analysis

Age: Four-year-olds have been easily the most successful age group during the past decade, winning four of the last five renewals.

Weight/Rating: Only two recent winners were rated below 85. This is not a race for workaday handicappers.

Form: This is best left to lightly-raced types – eight had a maximum of three starts beforehand – who won during their preparation.

Latest start: Six had their latest start over 12-14 furlongs during May. Do not be afraid to support those who have been sharpened by a run over middle-distances.
Another useful pointer is that five completed their preparation at Ascot, four taking part in the Royal Meeting.

Betting: Second favourites have a better record than favourites. However, as Quick Ransom (25/1), Bold Gait (12/1) and Cyrian (12/1) prove, shocks can occur.

Top trainers: Martin Pipe loves to have a pop at this race and has saddled two winners and two placed horses since 1990.
Paul Cole is another trainer to note, his record reading two wins (in the past three years) and one placed horse.

CURRAGH, SUNDAY JULY 2
IRISH DERBY (GROUP 1) THREE-YEAR-OLD COLTS AND FILLIES (1m 4f)

YR	FORM	WINNER	WT	S.P.	GOING	TRAINER	JOCKEY	FORM IN YEAR WN-RN	WN DIST.
90	121-111	**SALSABIL**	9.00	11-4(SF)	GD-SFT	J.Dunlop	W.Carson	3-3	7,8,12f
91	3011-41	**GENEROUS**	9.00	EV F	GD-SFT	P.Cole	A.Munro	1-2	12f
92	114-412	**ST JOVITE**	9.00	7-2(SF)	GD	J.Bolger(IR)	C.Roche	1-3	10f
93	-1111	**COMMANDER IN CHIEF**	9.00	4-7F	GD	H.Cecil	Pat Eddery	4-4	10,12f
94	11-21	**BALANCHINE**	8.11	5-1	GD-SFT	H.Ibrahim	L.Dettori	1-2	12f
95	01-2213	**WINGED LOVE**	9.00	5-1(SF)	GD-FM	A.Fabre(FR)	O.Peslier	1-4	10f
96	-12	**ZAGREB**	9.00	20-1	GD	D.Weld(IR)	P.Shanahan	1-2	10f
97	10-2114	**DESERT KING**	9.00	11-2	YDG	A.O'Brien(IR)	C.Roche	2-4	7,8f
98	-2211	**DREAM WELL**	9.00	2-1F	HVY	P.Bary(FR)	C.Asmussen	2-4	12f
99	11-121	**MONTJEU**	9.00	13-8F	GD	J.Hammon(FR)	C.Asmussen	2-3	10,12f

FAVOURITES/SECOND FAVOURITES (strike rate and to a £1 stake): Favs. 40 per cent, -£0.81, **S.Favs. 27 per cent, +£3.25.**

Introduction

In some ways this race is more informative than the Epsom Derby. After all, since 1990 it has attracted the outstanding French colts Dream Well and Montjeu, plus two crack fillies in Salsabil and Balanchine.

Ten year analysis

Form: While two-year-old form is no guide – three were unraced at that age – your selection must be established in the top class. To that end, seven won a Group One race during their preparation.

Latest start: Eight had their latest start in a 12-furlong Classic. Salsabil and Balanchine won the Oaks, Generous and Commander in Chief landed the Epsom Derby, while Dream Well and Montjeu followed suit in the French equivalent.
St Jovite (second in the Epsom Derby) and Winged Love (third in the French Derby) complete our octet.

Best trial: It is worth noting that no horse has completed the English-Irish Derby double since Commander in Chief seven seasons ago. By contrast, the last two French Derby heroes (Dream Well and Montjeu) both came on to score on The Curragh.

Betting: Four favourites and three second favourites have won during the past ten seasons. The market is a fair guide.

SANDOWN, FRIDAY JULY 7
HONG KONG JOCKEY CLUB TROPHY HANDICAP (1m 2f)

YR	FORM IN YEAR FORM	WINNERS	AGE-WT	RATING	S.P.	DRAW	GOING	TRAINER	JOCKEY	WN-RN	WN DIST.
90	140-012	**BOLD FOX**	4 9.05	98	12-1	11	GD-FM	G.Harwood	R.Cochrane	1-3	12f
91	410001	**YOU KNOW THE RULES**	4 7.12	80	14-1	3	GD	M.Channon	C.Rutter	2-7	8,9f
92	04-0322	**FIRE TOP**	7 8.09	91	14-1	18	SFT	R.Akehurst	T.Quinn	0-4	
93	211121	**SMARGINATO**	3 8.10	96	12-1	16	GD-FM	J.Dunlop	G.Carter	4-6	8f
94	2100-02	**KNOWTH**	5 7.08	75	13-2F	18	GD-FM	R.Akehurst	J.Quinn	0-2	
95	3-30311	**YOUSH**	3 8.01	87	6-1F	11	GD-FM	M.Jarvis	B.Doyle	2-5	10f
96	010-003	**SHEER DANZIG**	4 8.07	85	10-1	5	GD-SFT	R.Armstrong	W.Woods	0-3	
97	NO RACE										
98	3003-31	**YAVANA'S PACE**	6 8.03	8[illegible]	20-1	19	GD	M.Johnston	W.Lai	1-2	10f
99	01-2131	**MOUTAHDDEE**	3 8.02	9[illegible]	10-1	2	GD	M.Tregoning	T.Sprake	2-4	10f

AGE (wins-runners): **3-Y-O: 3-35**, 4-Y-O: 3-74, 5-Y-O: [illegible]-30, 6-Y-O+: 2-35.

FAVOURITES/SECOND FAVOURITES (strike rate and to a £1 stake): **Favs. 22 per cent, +£5.50,** S.Favs. 0 per cent, -£14.

AVERAGE WINNING RATING: 89.

Introduction

This has thrown up some smart winners - Bold Fox, Fire Top, Smarginato, Sheer Danzig, Yavana's Pace and Moutahddee were Group or Listed class – and is an outstanding handicap.

Ten year analysis

Age: Three-year-olds have the best strike rate, but age is no bar to success.

Weight/Rating: This is a tough race to win under a big weight – only Bold Fox has carried more than 8st 10lbs to victory since 1990.

Draw: While a low draw is not disastrous, high numbers seem to have a slight advantage. Six of the nine winners since 1990 came from stalls 11-19.

Form: Six won a handicap from May. This is not a race for inexperienced types who come here boasting an impressive maiden-race success.

Latest start: Five won and three finished second on their most recent outing. Avoid horses that disappointed last time.

Betting: Favourites boast a level-stakes profit but, with seven of the winners being priced between 10/1 and 20/1, it could pay to look for some value.

SANDOWN, SATURDAY JULY 8
CORAL-ECLIPSE STAKES (GROUP 1) (1m 2f)

YR	FORM	WINNERS	AGE-WT	RATING	S.P.	DRAW	GOING	TRAINER	JOCKEY	FORM IN YEAR WN-RN	WN DIST.
90	11-1023	**ELMAAMUL**	3 8.10	-	13-2	8	GD-FM	W.Hern	W.Carson	1-4	8f
91	01-3010	**ENVIRONMENT FRIEND**	3 8.10	-	28-1	4	GD	J.Fanshawe	G.Duffield	1-4	10.5f
92	1120-01(D)	**KOOYONGA**	4 9.04	123	7-2F	6	SFT	M.Kauntze(IR)	W.O'Connor	0-2	
93	0231-21	**OPERA HOUSE**	5 9.07	123	9-2	2	GD-FM	Sir M.Stoute	M.Kinane	1-2	12f
94	020-032	**EZZOUD**	5 9.07	120	5-1(SF)	6	GD-FM	Sir M.Stoute	W.Swinburn	0-3	
95	1111-11	**HALLING**	4 9.07	-	7-1	3	GD-FM	S.Bin Suroor	W.Swinburn	2-2	8,10f
96	110-101	**HALLING**	5 9.07	128	10-3(SF)	1	GD-SFT	S.Bin Suroor	J.Reid	2-3	9,10f
97	1121-32	**PILSUDSKI**	5 9.07	126	11-2(SF)	1	GD-SFT	Sir M.Stoute	M.Kinane	0-2	
98	1323-12	**DAYLAMI**	4 9.07	122	6-4F	5	GD	S.Bin Suroor	L.Dettori	1-2	10f
99	212-100	**COMPTON ADMIRAL**	3 8.10	111	20-1	7	GD-FM	G.Butler	D.Holland	1-3	8f

D = Disqualified

AGE (wins-runners): 3-Y-O: 3-22, 4-Y-O: 3-31, **5-Y-O: 4-14,** 6-Y-O+: 0-10.
FAVOURITES/SECOND FAVOURITES (strike rate and to a £1 stake): Favs. 20 per cent, -£3, **S.Favs. 21 per cent, +£2.83.**
AVERAGE WINNING RATING: 122.
TOP TRAINER (wins-runners, strike rate and to a £1 stake): **Sir Michael Stoute (3-11, 27 per cent, +£7). Saeed Bin Suroor (3-8, 37 per cent, +£6.83)**

Introduction

This is usually the first opportunity we have to compare the best of the Classic generation with their elders. Compton Admiral struck a blow for the youngsters last term but, in general, the 'oldies' have dominated recently.

Ten year analysis

Age: Older horses have a seven-three advantage over their three-year-old rivals since 1990.

Weight/Rating: Only Compton Admiral (111) was rated below 120. This is a race for established performers.

Form: All ten had a two-four race preparation, eight winning. Underlining the 'established' feel of this race, five won and three made the frame in a Group One or Two event beforehand.
Note that all successful three-year-olds ran in the Epsom Derby, Elmaamul finishing third while Environment Friend and Compton Admiral were unplaced.

Latest start: Nine ran in a Group One or Two event on their latest start, eight at Epsom's Derby Meeting or Royal Ascot. That seems the ideal preparation for a potential Eclipse winner.

Betting: Second favourites have a better record than favourites. However, outsiders can pop up, witness Environment Friend (28/1) and Compton Admiral (20/1).

Top trainers: Sir Michael Stoute has an excellent record, but Saeed Bin Suroor and the Godolphin team have made this race their own recently.
Over the past five seasons Sheikh Mohammed's stable has saddled three winners and four placed horses.

HAYDOCK, SATURDAY JULY 8
OLD NEWTON CUP HANDICAP (0-110) (1m 4f)

YR	FORM	WINNERS	AGE-WT	RATING	S.P.	DRAW	GOING	TRAINER	JOCKEY	FORM IN YEAR WN-RN	WN DIST.
90	1-12131	**HATEEL**	4 9.06	98	4-1	6	SFT	P.Walwyn	L.Dettori	3-5	11,12f
91	110-011	**LIBK**	3 8.11	93	5-1(SF)	2	GD-FM	H.T.Jones	R.Hills	2-3	11,12f
92	230-113	**MATADOR**	5 9.02	96	11-4F	5	GD-SFT	R.Charlton	Pat Eddery	2-3	12f
93	0-00100	**GLIDE PATH**	4 8.02	74	20-1	5	GD	J.Hills	R.Hills	1-5	12f
94	200-020	**GLIDE PATH**	5 8.10	85	10-1	1	GD-FM	J.Hills	M.Hills	0-3	
95	21020-4	**LOMBARDIC**	4 8.12	87	10-1	1	GD-FM	J.Cecil	J.Reid	0-1	
96	0420/12	**KEY TO MY HEART**	6 10.00	110	9-2(SF)	2	GD	S.Hall	R.Hughes	1-2	10f
97	12/00-01	**ZARALASKA**	6 9.08	103	5-1(SF)	13	GD	L.Cumani	Pat Eddery	1-2	12f
98	110-000	**PERFECT PARADIGM**	4 9.02	94	14-1	7	GD-FM	J.Gosden	G.Hind	0-3	
99	0-12210	**CELESTIAL WELCOME**	4 8.10	85	16-1	1	GD-SFT	M.Reveley	C.Lowther	2-5	8,10f

AGE (wins-runners): 3-Y-O: 1-27, **4-Y-O: 5-37**, 5-Y-O: 2-22, 6-Y-O+: 3-23.
FAVOURITES/SECOND FAVOURITES (strike rate and to a £1 stake): Favs. 9 per cent, -£7.25, **S.Favs. 23 per cent, +£4.50.**
AVERAGE WINNING RATING: 92.

Introduction

As can be gauged from the impressive average win rating, this is no ordinary handicap. Hateel, Libk, Matador, Key To My Heart and Zaralaska were class acts, and your selection should be better than an everyday handicapper.

Ten year analysis

Age: Three-year-olds have a modest record and should be treated with a degree of caution. By contrast, four-year-olds boast an excellent strike rate and should continue to perform well.

Weight/Rating: Only one of the last ten carried less than 8st 10lbs or was rated below 85. This is a race for those in the top half of the handicap.

Form: Seven won over 10-12 furlongs from May, six landing a handicap. It is also worth noting that seven had a maximum of three starts during their preparation. Look for lightly-raced types.

Latest start: Good recent form is irrelevant – four were unplaced on their latest start – and it is more significant that seven completed their preparation in a decent handicap during June.

Best trial: Royal Ascot's Duke Of Edinburgh Handicap (formerly the Bessborough) has been a sound pointer. Four ran in that contest, Hateel and Zaralaska winning, Matador finishing third and Glide Path unplaced.

Betting: Favourites have a dismal record, particularly when compared with the level-stakes profit and 23 per cent strike rate of second favourites.
That said, with recent winners returning at 10/1(twice), 14/1, 16/1 and 20/1, it could pay to look for some value.

NEWMARKET, TUESDAY JULY 11
PRINCESS OF WALES'S STAKES (GROUP 2) (1m 4f)

YR	FORM	WINNERS	AGE-WT	RATING	S.P.	DRAW	GOING	TRAINER	JOCKEY	FORM IN YEAR WN-RN	WN DIST.
90	1220-22	**SAPIENCE**	4 9.00	112	11-2	4	GD	J.FitzGerald	Pat Eddery	0-2	
91	1-11312	**ROCK HOPPER**	4 9.03	-	4-6F	6	GD	Sir M.Stoute	Pat Eddery	3-5	12f
92	220-111	**SADDLERS' HALL**	4 9.05	119	4-7F	2	GD	Sir M.Stoute	Pat Eddery	3-3	12,13f
93	12-2300	**DESERT TEAM**	3 8.01	-	10-1	7	GD-FM	J.Bolger(IR)	W.Carson	0-4	
94	2102-23	**WAGON MASTER**	4 9.00	104	7-1	7	GD-FM	A.Stewart	R.Hills	0-2	
95	00-3311	**BEAUCHAMP HERO**	5 9.09	105	8-1	6	GD-FM	J.Dunlop	J.Reid	2-4	12f
96	0110-33	**POSIDONAS**	4 9.07	116	20-1	6	GD	P.Cole	T.Quinn	0-2	
97	21114-1	**SHANTOU**	4 9.07	123	11-4(SF)	7	GD	J.Gosden	L.Dettori	1-1	12f
98	32-3002	**FRUITS OF LOVE**	3 8.03	107	7-1	3	GD-FM	M.Johnston	M.Hills	0-4	
99	104/141-	**CRAIGSTEEL**	4 9.02	111	13-2(SF)	6	GD	H.Cecil	K.Fallon	0-0	

AGE (wins-runners): 3-Y-O: 2-11, **4-Y-O: 7-37,** 5-Y-O: 1-21, 6-Y-O+: 0-5.
FAVOURITES/SECOND FAVOURITES (strike rate and to a £1 stake): Favs. 17 per cent, -£8.77, **S.Favs. 20 per cent, +£1.25.**
AVERAGE WINNING RATING: 112

Introduction

This is best left to middle-distance stayers who fall fractionally short of the top class. Rock Hopper, Saddlers' Hall, Posidonas, Fruits of Love and Craigsteel are good examples of the type of horse to look for.

Ten year analysis

Age: Four-year-olds have an excellent record and should be favoured.

Weight/Rating: The average win rating (112) is relatively low. That score is dragged down by horses like Wagon Master (104), Beauchamp Hero (105) and Fruits Of Love (107), demonstrating that apparently ordinary horses can score.

Form: A recent victory is not necessary – six failed to score earlier in their year – and it is more important to note that four won and three were placed in a Group One or Two beforehand.

Latest start: Eight ran in a Group race from May on their latest start, three winning and four making the frame.

Best trial: Four ran in Royal Ascot's Hardwicke Stakes, Rock Hopper and Beauchamp Hero winning, while Wagon Master and Posidonas finished third.

Betting: Second favourites have been more successful than favourites, although the market is not a great guide.

NEWMARKET, TUESDAY JULY 11
CHERRY HINTON STAKES TWO-YEAR-OLD FILLIES (GROUP 2) (6f)

YR	FORM	WINNERS	WT	S.P.	DRAW	GOING	TRAINER	JOCKEY	FORM IN YEAR WN-RN	WN DIST.
90	11	**CHICARICA**	8.12	9-4F	4	GD	J.Gosden	W.Swinburn	2-2	6f
91	11	**MUSICALE**	8.09	9-2	5	GD	H.Cecil	S.Cauthen	2-2	6,7f
92	2	**SAYYEDATI**	8.09	6-4F	7	GD	C.Brittain	M.Roberts	0-1	
93	11	**LEMON SOUFFLE**	8.09	5-4F	8	GD-FM	R.Hannon	L.Piggott	2-2	5,6f
94	1	**RED CARNIVAL**	8.09	11-4(SF)	6	GD-FM	Sir M.Stoute	W.Swinburn	1-1	5f
95	12	**APPLAUD**	8.09	11-2	4	GD-FM	D.Loder	Pat Eddery	1-2	5f
96	1	**DAZZLE**	8.09	2-1F	3	GD	Sir M.Stoute	K.Fallon	1-1	5f
97	21	**ASFURAH**	8.09	9-2(SF)	2	GD	S.Bin Suroor	L.Dettori	1-2	5f
98	421	**WANNABE GRAND**	8.09	11-1	7	GD-FM	J.Noseda	W.Swinburn	1-3	6f
99	10	**TORGAU**	8.09	12-1	7	GD	G.Bravery	G.Stevens	1-2	5f

FAVOURITES/SECOND FAVOURITES (strike rate and to a £1 stake): **Favs. 40 per cent, +£1**, S.Favs. 20 per cent,-£3.

Introduction

This race has a mixed record as a long-term guide. While Sayyedati and Lemon Souffle went on to win in the highest grade as three-year-olds, Kerrera, Musicale and Dazzle proved disappointing

Ten year analysis

Weight/Rating: Only one of the last ten – Chicarica – carried a 3lb penalty. This is a race for unpenalised runners.

Form: None had run more than twice – only one made her debut before May – nine winning, eight from June.
Remember that seven unbeaten fillies have landed this prize in the past decade.

Latest start: Six won on their latest start. However, it is more interesting to note that five completed their preparation at Royal Ascot, where three won and one finished second.

Best trial: Three ran in Royal Ascot's Windsor Castle Stakes, Dazzle and Asfurah winning while Applaud finished second.

Betting: Favourites have a useful 40 per cent strike rate, although the last two winners have returned at 11/1 and 12/1.

Top trainer: Sir Michael Stoute is not renowned for producing precocious juveniles. That said, he has still managed to send out two winners and two placed horses since 1990.

NEWMARKET, WEDNESDAY JULY 12
FALMOUTH STAKES (GROUP 2) FILLIES AND MARES (1m)

YR	FORM	WINNERS	AGE-WT	RATING	S.P.	DRAW	GOING	TRAINER	JOCKEY	FORM IN YEAR WN-RN	WN DIST.
90	1113-41	**CHIMES OF FREEDOM**	3 8.12	-	4-6F	3	GD-FM	H.Cecil	S.Cauthen	1-2	8f
91	0-00000	**ONLY YOURS**	3 8.06	110	10-1	4	GD	R.Hannon	M.Roberts	0-5	
92	340-000	**GUSSY MARLOWE**	4 9.01	118	7-1	7	GD	C.Brittain	M.Roberts	0-3	
93	4310-12	**NICHE**	3 8.06	116	13-8F	2	GD-FM	R.Hannon	L.Piggott	1-2	7f
94	11113-4	**LEMON SOUFFLE**	3 8.06	118	6-5F	2	GD-FM	R.Hannon	L.Piggott	0-1	
95	3-20	**CARAMBA**	3 8.06	-	5-2	3	GD-FM	R.Hannon	M.Roberts	0-2	
96	-111	**SENSATION**	3 8.06	-	10-11F	7	GD	C.Head(FR)	M.Kinane	3-3	8f
97	121-44	**RYAFAN**	3 8.06	113	4-1	3	GD-FM	J.Gosden	Pat Eddery	0-2	
98	2-013	**LOVERS KNOT**	3 8.06	93	11-4F	3	GD-FM	Sir M.Stoute	J. Reid	1-3	7f
99	130-221	**RONDA**	3 8.06	-	8-1	7	GD	C.Laffon-Parias(FR)	D.Boeuf	1-3	11f

AGE (wins-runners): **3-Y-O: 9-61,** 4-Y-O: 1-14, 5-Y-O: 0-2, 6-Y-O+: 0-0.
FAVOURITES/SECOND FAVOURITES (strike rate and to a £1 stake): **Favs. 45 per cent, +£0.14,** S.Favs. 0 per cent, -£11.
AVERAGE WINNING RATING: 111.
TOP TRAINER (wins-runners, strike rate and to a £1 stake): **Richard Hannon (4-4, 100 per cent, +£15.32).**

Introduction

While this has fallen to some smart fillies – Niche and Lemon Souffle being recent examples – most recent winners fell below the top-class.

Ten year analysis

Age: Three-year-olds dominate this race and should be followed.

Weight/Rating: Only one of the last ten carried the penalty for a Group One or Two success. This is another race for unpenalised runners.

Form: Eight had a maximum of three starts beforehand and lightly-raced fillies have the edge.
Four won a Group race beforehand (three landed Group Threes, four others making the frame in that sphere). Avoid any stepping straight out of the minor leagues.

Latest start: Nine ran in a Group race from June on their latest start, three winning and three making the frame.

Betting: While second favourites have drawn a blank since 1990, favourites boast a useful 45 per cent strike rate. The market is a fair guide.

Top trainer: Richard Hannon has a flawless record – four winners from four runners – and must be followed closely.

NEWMARKET, THURSDAY JULY 13
JULY CUP (GROUP 1) (6f)

YR	FORM	WINNER	AGE-WT	RATING	S.P.	DRAW	GOING	TRAINER	JOCKEY	FORM IN YEAR WN-RN	WN DIST.
90	10-12	**ROYAL ACADEMY**	3 8.13	-	7-1	3	GD-FM	M.V.O'Brien(IR)	J.Reid	1-2	7f
91	2210-11	**POLISH PATRIOT**	3 8.13	-	6-1	4	GD-FM	G.Harwood	R.Cochrane	2-2	6f
92	102-122	**MR BROOKS**	5 9.06	-	16-1	6	GD	R.Hannon	L.Piggott	1-3	5f
93	01-0100	**HAMAS**	4 9.06	113	33-1	9	GD-FM	P.Walwyn	W.Carson	1-4	6f
94	112-011	**OWINGTON**	3 8.13	117	3-1(SF)	1	GD	G.Wragg	Paul Eddery	2-3	6f
95	411-112	**LAKE CONISTON**	4 9.06	120	13-8F	9	GD-FM	G.Lewis	Pat Eddery	2-3	6f
96	03-1111	**ANABAA**	4 9.05	-	11-4(SF)	2	GD-FM	C.Head(FR)	F.Head	4-4	5,5.5f
97	2122-20	**COMPTON PLACE**	3 8.13	111	50-1	1	GD-FM	J.Toller	S.Sanders	0-2	
98	1114-23	**ELNADIM**	4 9.05	121	3-1F	18	FM	J.Dunlop	R.Hills	0-2	
99	1*23-24	**STRAVINSKY**	3 8.13	113	8-1	6	GD-FM	A.O'Brien(IR)	M.Kinane	0-2	

*Disqualified

AGE (wins-runners): 3-Y-O: 5-49, **4-Y-O: 4-37**, 5-Y-O: 1-15, 6-Y-O+: 0-7.
FAVOURITES/SECOND FAVOURITES (strike rate and to a £1 stake): Favs. 20 per cent, -£3.38, S.Favs. 18 per cent, -£3.25.
AVERAGE WINNING RATING: 116.

Introduction

This race witnessed an exceptional performance from Stravinsky last season and must be recognised as our premier six-furlong event.

Ten year analysis

Age: Three and four-year-olds have ruled the roost for some time and should continue to dominate.

Weight/Rating: Surprisingly, three recent winners – Hamas, Compton Place and Stravinsky – had modest ratings when landing this prize. Do not be afraid to support an improver.

Form: Seven won beforehand, six landing a Group race. Indeed, only Compton Place failed to make the frame in that sphere during his preparation.

Latest start: Seven completed their build-up by running at Royal Ascot (six over five or six furlongs), where two won, three made the frame and two were unplaced.

Best trials: The Cork And Orrery Stakes is the pick of our Royal Ascot trials. Four ran in that race, Polish Patriot and Owington winning, Lake Coniston finishing second and Hamas unplaced. Even more useful is the Duke Of York Stakes. Five used that race as part of their preparation, Hamas, Owington and Lake Coniston winning, while Mr Brooks and Elnadim finished second.

Betting: This has been something of a bookies' benefit in recent seasons – winners were returned at 16/1, 33/1 and 50/1 – and the market is a poor guide.

NEWMARKET, THURSDAY JULY 13
BUNBURY CUP HANDICAP (0-105) (7f)

YR	FORM	WINNER	AGE-WT	RATING	S.P.	DRAW	GOING	TRAINER	JOCKEY	FORM IN YEAR WN-RN	WN DIST.
90	0/1-0010	**FEDORIA**	4 8.03	82	8-1(SF)	8	GD	M.Jarvis	L.Dettori	1-4	7f
91	-1210	**SAVOYARD**	3 9.00	101	16-1	11	GD	M.Jarvis	W.Swinburn	2-4	7f
92	210-20	**CONSIGLIERE**	4 9.01	85	10-1	5	GD	R.Charlton	Paul Eddery	0-2	
93	033213	**EN ATTENDANT**	5 9.04	90	14-1	4	GD-FM	B.Hanbury	L.Piggott	1-6	7f
94	3030-00	**EN ATTENDANT**	6 9.12	90	14-1	7	GD	B.Hanbury	L.Piggott	0-2	
95	0010-02	**CADEAUX TRYST**	3 9.01	97	20-1	17	GD-FM	E.Dunlop	W.Swinburn	0-2	
96	0000-33	**CRUMPTON HILL**	4 8.12	86	7-1F	3	GD-FM	N.Graham	M.Roberts	0-2	
97	300220	**TUMBLEWEED RIDGE**	4 9.06	94	20-1	19	GD-FM	B.Meehan	M.Tebbutt	0-6	
98	120-10	**HO LENG**	3 9.07	14-1	102	20	FM	L.Perratt	M.Kinane	1-2	7f
99	104-302	**GRANGEVILLE**	4 9.03	92	13-2JF	20	GD-FM	I.Balding	K.Fallon	0-3	

AGE (wins-runners): **3-Y-O: 3-24**, 4-Y-O: 5-86, 5-Y-O: 1-41, 6-Y-O+: 1-46.
FAVOURITES/SECOND FAVOURITES (strike rate and to a £1 stake): Favs. 10 per cent, -£2.50, **S.Favs. 15 per cent, +£4.**
AVERAGE WINNING RATING: 93.

Introduction

There are always a few hard luck stories in this rough-and-tumble handicap, but the cream usually rises to the top. Smart horses like Savoyard, Consigliere, En Attendant, Cadeaux Tryst, Tumbleweed Ridge and Grangeville figure among the last ten winners.

Ten year analysis

Age: Three and four-year-olds have a better strike rate than their older rivals.

Weight/Rating: High-weights have an excellent record. None of the last nine carried less than 8st 12lbs.

Draw: Those drawn high have had the edge recently, although low numbers did well in the early nineties.

Form: Eight had a two-four start preparation, four winning and four making the frame over seven furlongs or a mile from May.

Latest start: Perhaps the most important statistic is that seven ran at Royal Ascot on their latest start, one making the frame and six finishing unplaced.

Betting: Grangeville broke an 11-year losing run for favourites when winning last season. This race has not been kind to market leaders.

Top trainer: There are no outstanding training trends, although Ben Hanbury managed to score twice through his stable stalwart En Attendant.

YORK, SATURDAY JULY 15
JOHN SMITH'S CUP HANDICAP (0-110) (1m 2f 85y)

YR	FORM	WINNER	AGE-WT	RATING	S.P.	DRAW	GOING	TRAINER	JOCKEY	FORM IN YEAR WN-RN	WN DIST.
90	020-111	**ERADICATE**	5 9.04	99	15-2	9	GD-FM	P.Calver	W.Newnes	3-3	10f
91	10-3424	**HALKOPOUS**	5 7.03	73	7-2F	7	GD	M.Tompkins	F.Norton	0-4	
92	434-111	**MR CONFUSION**	4 8.03	83	8-1	14	GD-SFT	S.Norton	O.Pears	3-3	10f
93	33-212	**BARON FERDINAND**	3 8.09	92	4-1JF	1	GD-FM	R.Charlton	R.Cochrane	1-3	10f
94	1-11114	**CEZANNE**	5 9.12	105	9-2(SF)	3	GD-FM	H.Ibrahim	G.Hind	4-5	9,10,12f
95	10130-4	**NAKED WELCOME**	3 8.04	90	6-1(SF)	9	GD-FM	M.F-Godley	D.Holland	0-1	
96	102-000	**WILCUMA**	5 9.02	89	10-1	2	GD	P.Makin	Pat Eddery	0-3	
97	020311-	**PASTERNAK**	4 8.03	85	13-2(SF)	1	GD	Sir M.Prescott	G.Duffield	0-0	
98	04-331	**PORTO FORICOS**	3 8.03	90	6-1	7	FM	H.Cecil	J.Quinn	1-3	9f
99	00-0210	**ACHILLES**	4 8.11	90	25-1	6	GD-FM	K.Burke	J.Weaver	1-4	12f

AGE (wins-runners): **3-Y-O: 3-34,** 4-Y-O: 3-63, 5-Y-O: 4-40, 6-Y-O+: 0-29.
FAVOURITES/SECOND FAVOURITES (strike rate and to a £1 stake): Favs. 13 per cent, -£5.50, **S.Favs. 21 per cent, +£6.**
AVERAGE WINNING RATING: 90.

Introduction

This is a red-hot handicap with an active ante-post market. Eradicate, Baron Ferdinand, Cezanne, Naked Welcome and Pasternak are outstanding recent winners and it will take an above-average performer to follow their lead.

Ten year analysis

Age: It is 30 years since a horse aged six or above (My Swanee in 1969) scored. Stick with younger runners.

Weight/Rating: Only one of the winners - Halkopous - was rated below 83.

Form: Seven had a maximum of three starts beforehand and this is best left to relatively unexposed horses. Six scored during their preparation, five around a mile and a quarter.

Latest start: Eight had their latest start in a 10-12 furlong handicap, two winning and four making the frame.

Best trial: There are no outstanding trials, although three of the last six took part in the Hong Kong Jockey Club Trophy Handicap (run at Sandown's Eclipse Meeting in early July). Keep an eye on those who had a crack at that valuable prize.

Betting: Achilles (25/1) is the only winning outsider and, while favourites have shown a level-stakes loss, this is best left to fancied horses.

CURRAGH, SUNDAY JULY 16
IRISH OAKS (GROUP 1) THREE-YEAR-OLD FILLIES (1m 4f)

YR	FORM	WINNER	WT	S.P.	GOING	TRAINER	JOCKEY	FORM IN YEAR WN-RN	WN DIST.
90	212-23	**KNIGHT'S BARONESS**	9.00	13-8F	GD-FM	P.Cole	T.Quinn	0-2	
91	1-111	**POSSESSIVE DANCER**	9.00	8-1	GD-FM	A.Scott	S.Cauthen	3-3	8,9,12f
92	-111	**USER FRIENDLY**	9.00	8-11F	GD-SFT	C.Brittain	G.Duffield	3-3	10,12f
93	1-1101	**WEMYSS BIGHT**	9.00	9-2(SF)	GD-SFT	A.Fabre(FR)	Pat Eddery	3-4	10,12f
94	0-11	**BOLAS**	9.00	5-2F	SFT	B.Hills	Pat Eddery	2-2	11,12f
95	1314-13	**PURE GRAIN**	9.00	9-2	SFT	M.Stoute	J.Reid	1-2	10f
96	144-231	**DANCE DESIGN**	9.00	9-2(SF)	GD-FM	D.Weld(IR)	M.Kinane	1-3	10f
97	-130	**EBADIYLA**	9.00	9-2(SF)	GD-FM	J.Oxx(IR)	J.Murtagh	1-3	10f
98	1020-43	**WINONA**	9.00	12-1	GD-FM	J.Oxx(IR)	J.Murtagh	0-2	
99	32-111	**RAMRUMA**	9.00	4-9F	GD-FM	H.Cecil	Pat Eddery	3-3	12f

FAVOURITES/SECOND FAVOURITES (strike rate and to a £1 stake): Favs. 40 per cent, -£0.71, **S.Favs. 30 per cent, +£6.50.**

Introduction

While there is an argument for suggesting the Irish Derby is a more interesting race than its Epsom counterpart, that hardly seems the case here. Possessive Dancer, Bolas and Winona were sub-standard Classic winners.

Ten year analysis

Form: Smart two-year-old form is not essential – four failed to score at that age.
Seven won a 10-12 furlong Group race earlier in their year, while it is worth noting that only two took part in a mile Classic.

Latest start: Nine ran in a Group race during June on their latest start, six winning and three making the frame.

Best trial: Six of the last ten ran in the Epsom Oaks, User Friendly and Ramruma winning, Knight's Baroness and Pure Grain finishing third, while Wemyss Bight and Ebadiyla were unplaced.

Betting: Favourites and second favourites have won seven of the last ten runnings. The market can be followed with some confidence.

Top trainers: The Irish have only managed to keep this prize at home three times since 1990. John Oxx was responsible for two of those successes and is obviously a man to respect. However, six English fillies have been successful and the raiding party are usually difficult to stop.

NEWBURY, SATURDAY JULY 22
*WEATHERBYS SUPER SPRINT TWO-YEAR-OLDS (5f)

YR	FORM	WINNER	WT	S.P.	DRAW	GOING	TRAINER	JOCKEY	FORM IN YEAR WN-RN	WN DIST.
91	1112	**PARIS HOUSE**	8.03	5-4F	2	GD-SFT	J.Berry	J.Carroll	3-4	5
92	111	**LYRIC FANTASY**	8.11	2-5F	11	GD-SFT	R.Hannon	M.Roberts	3-3	5f
93	1121	**RISKY**	8.10	8-11F	14	GD	R.Hannon	W.Swinburn	3-4	5f
94	11	**BRIEF GLIMPSE**	8.01	7-2(SF)	2	GD-FM	D.Chappell	M.Hills	2-2	6f
95	1	**BLUE IRIS**	8.01	13-2	16	GD	M.Jarvis	W.Carson	1-1	5f
96	01	**MISS STAMPER**	8.02	14-1	3	GD-FM	R.Hannon	D.Harrison	1-2	5f
97	414	**LORD KINTYRE**	8.07	7-1	23	GD-FM	B.R.Millman	B.Doyle	1-3	6f
98	111	**FLANDERS**	8.11	6-5F	18	GD-FM	T.D.Easterby	L.Charnock	3-3	5f
99	310	**DON PUCCINI**	8.11	10-1	22	GD-FM	B.Smart	J.Stack	1-3	6f

*NO RACE 1990.

FAVOURITES/SECOND FAVOURITES (strike rate and to a £1 stake): **Favs. 44 per cent, -£1.42.** S.Favs. 9 per cent, -£6.50.

TOP TRAINER (wins-runners, strike rate and to a £1 stake): **Richard Hannon (3-32, 9 per cent, -£13.82).**

Introduction

It takes an exceptionally speedy juvenile to win this valuable heat. Paris House, Risky, Lyric Fantasy, Lord Kintyre and Flanders were high-class two-year-olds.

Ten year analysis

Weight/Rating: None of the winners carried more than 8st 11lbs.

Draw: While low numbers can win, high draws have had the best of the argument recently. Four of the last five came from stalls 16-23.

Form: All nine scored beforehand, seven during June. Avoid inconsistent types – only two finished out of the frame during their preparation.

Latest start: Six won on their latest start, but it is more interesting to note that the same number completed their preparation at Royal Ascot (three won, two placed and one unplaced). Anything with form at the Royal Meeting must be treated with respect.

Best trial: There are no outstanding trials, although the Windsor Castle Stakes and Queen Mary Stakes are the pick of the Royal Ascot pointers.

Top trainer: Richard Hannon usually sends a posse in pursuit of this prize, his 32 runners to date yielding three winners and seven placed horses.

ASCOT, SATURDAY JULY 29
KING GEORGE VI AND THE QUEEN ELIZABETH DIAMOND STAKES (GROUP 1) (1m 4f)

YR	FORM	WINNER	AGE-WT	RATING	S.P.	DRAW	GOING	TRAINER	JOCKEY	FORM IN YEAR WN-RN	WN DIST.
90	1-113	**BELMEZ**	3 8.09	-	15-2	11	GD-FM	H.Cecil	M.J.Kinane	2-3	11,12f
91	011-411	**GENEROUS**	3 8.09	-	4-6F	4	GD	P.Cole	A.Munro	2-3	12f
92	14-4121	**ST JOVITE**	3 8.09	-	4-5F	2	GD-FM	J.Bolger(IR)	S.Craine	2-4	10,12f
93	231-211	**OPERA HOUSE**	5 9.07	123	8-1	2	GD	Sir M.Stoute	M.Roberts	2-3	10,12f
94	1-10422	**KING'S THEATRE**	3 8.09	120	12-1	7	GD-FM	H.Cecil	M.Kinane	1-5	8f
95	1-1	**LAMMTARRA**	3 8.09	-	9-4F	3	GD-FM	S.Bin Suroor	L.Dettori	1-1	12f

96	1211-43	**PENTIRE**	4 9.07	126	10-3(SF)	7	GD-FM	G.Wragg	M.Hills	0-2	
97	12143-2	**SWAIN**	5 9.07	122	16-1	5	SFT	S.Bin Suroor	J.Reid	0-1	
98	130-223	**SWAIN**	6 9.07	127	11-2	5	GD-FM	S.Bin Suroor	L.Dettori	0-3	
99	413-021	**DAYLAMI**	5 9.07	125	3-1(SF)	8	GD-FM	S. Bin Suroor	L.Dettori	1-3	12f

AGE (wins-runners): **3-Y-O: 5-26,** 4-Y-O: 1-39, 5-Y-O: 3-16, 6-Y-O+: 1-8.
FAVOURITES\SECOND FAVOURITES (strike rate and to a £1 stake): Favs. 30 per cent, -£3.29, **S.Favs. 20 per cent, -£1.67.**
AVERAGE WINNING RATING: 124.
TOP TRAINER (wins-runs, strike rate and to a £1 stake): **Saeed Bin Suroor (4-10, 40 per cent, +£20.75).**

Introduction

Inaugurated in 1951, this is Britain's premier all-aged contest. The roll of honour reads like a who's who and features such luminaries as Ribot, Nijinsky, Mill Reef, Brigadier Gerard, Shergar, Dancing Brave, Swain and Daylami.

Ten year analysis

Age: Three-year-olds have a marginally better strike rate than five-year-olds. These appear the age groups to concentrate on.

Weight/Rating: As is borne out by our average win rating of 124, this is a race for proven Group One horses.

Form: Seven landed a Group race during their preparation, while all the successful three-year-olds took part in either the Epsom or Irish Derby, three winning and two making the frame. Note that only one – Swain in 1998 – competed at Royal Ascot.

Latest start: Eight ran in a Group One on their latest start, five winning and three making the frame.

Best trials: Four ran in the Epsom Derby, Generous and Lammtarra winning, while St Jovite and King's Theatre finished second. The Irish Derby boasts almost identical results, Generous and St Jovite coming home in front, Belmez and King's Theatre making the frame. Form in either – or both – of these races is essential for three-year-olds.

Betting: Favourites and second favourites have produced a level-stakes loss since 1990.

Top trainer: Saeed Bin Suroor and the Godolphin team have made this race their own in recent seasons, saddling four of the last five winners. Such a record cannot be ignored.

GOODWOOD, TUESDAY AUGUST 2
MARCHPOLE CUP HANDICAP (1m 2f)

YR	FORM	WINNER	AGE-WT	RATING	S.P.	DRAW	GOING	TRAINER	JOCKEY	FORM IN YEAR WN-RN	WN DIST.
90	401011	**SONG OF SIXPENCE**	6 9.05	93	9-2	5	GD-FM	I.Balding	C.Cauthen	4-8	10f
91	001-001	**IJTIHAAD**	4 9.05	90	11-2	1	GD-FM	W.Hern	W.Carson	1-3	10f
92	324101	**KNOCK KNOCK**	7 9.00	88	9-2F	3	GD-FM	I.Balding	R.Cochrane	2-8	10f
*93	30-0120	**ROSE ALTO**	5 8.13	89	25-1	8	GD-SFT	J.Fanshawe	G.Duffield	1-4	10f
94	302041	**DESERT SHOT**	4 8.13	104	12-1	9	FM	Sir M.Stoute	J.Tate	1-6	8f
95	02200-0	**SILVER GROOM**	5 7.06	65	6-1	12	FM	R.Akehurst	M.Henry	0-1	
96	0-40001	**GRAND SELECTION**	4 8.03	81	12-1	2	GD-FM	M.Bell	M.Fenton	1-5	10f
97	02-3101	**DANISH RHAPSODY**	4 8.06	90	14-1	11	GD-FM	Lady Herries	J.Reid	2-4	9,10f
98	2020-03	**SUPPLY AND DEMAND**	4 9.00	94	3-1F	8	GD-FM	G.L.Moore	K.Fallon	0-2	
99	100-000	**ORMELIE**	4 9.00	90	6-1	7	GD-FM	P.Chapple-Hyam	J.Fortune	0-3	

*KNOWTH 4 7.02, 16-1, R.Akehurst, D.Wright, finished first, disqualified and placed second.

AGE (wins-runners): 3-Y-O: 0-8, **4-Y-O: 6-56,** 5-Y-O: 2-25, 6-Y-O+: 2-34.

FAVOURITES\SECOND FAVOURITES (strike rate and to a £1 stake): Favs. **18 per cent, -£1.50,** S.Favs. 0 per cent, -£13.

AVERAGE WINNING RATING: 88.

Introduction

Formerly known as the Chesterfield Cup, this race numbers Song Of Sixpence, Desert Shot and Danish Rhapsody among its recent winners. That trio went on to land a Listed or Group event, which bodes well for the long-term future of their successor.

Ten year analysis

Age: Four-year-olds have the best strike rate, being responsible for five of the last six winners.

Weight/Rating: Our average win rating (88) is a fair guide to the level of ability required.

Form: Seven won earlier in their year, five landing a handicap around this ten-furlong trip.

Latest start: Six won on their most recent outing. However, it is more pertinent to note that eight completed their preparation in a handicap during July.

Betting: Favourites and second favourites have a dismal record. Outsiders have scored at 12/1 (twice), 14/1 and 25/1 and it often pays to look for some value.

Top trainer: Ian Balding enjoys having a crack at this race and has sent out two winners and a placed horse since 1990.

GOODWOOD, WEDNESDAY AUGUST 2
SUSSEX STAKES (GROUP 1) (1m)

YR	FORM	WINNER	AGE-WT	RATING	S.P.	DRAW	GOING	TRAINER	JOCKEY	FORM IN YEAR WN-RN	WN DIST.
90	131-232	**DISTANT RELATIVE**	4 9.07	124	4-1	8	GD	B.Hills	W.Carson	0-3	
91	-112	**SECOND SET**	3 8.13	-	5-1	8	GD	L.Cumani	L.Dettori	2-3	7,8f
92	111-211	**MARLING**	3 8.10	-	11-10F	7	GD-FM	G.Wragg	Pat Eddery	2-3	8f
93	2-11222	**BIGSTONE**	3 8.13	-	14-1	5	GD-SFT	E.Lellouche(FR)	D.Boeuf	2-5	8f
94	-2012	**DISTANT VIEW**	3 8.13	120	4-1(SF)	9	FM	H.Cecil	Pat Eddery	1-4	8f
95	4200-20	**SAYYEDATI**	5 9.04	120	11-2	4	FM	C.Brittain	B.Doyle	0-2	
96	2-13011	**FIRST ISLAND**	4 9.07	119	5-1(SF)	9	GD-FM	G.Wragg	M.Hills	3-5	8,10f
97	1-13231	**ALI-ROYAL**	4 9.07	120	13-2	3	GD-FM	H.Cecil	K.Fallon	2-5	8,9f
98	141-021	**AMONG MEN**	4 9.07	118	4-1(SF)	10	GD-SFT	Sir M.Stoute	M.Kinane	1-3	7f
99	111-2	**ALJABR**	3 8.13	120	11-10F	6	GD-FM	S.Bin Suroor	L.Dettori	0-1	

AGE (wins-runners): **3-Y-O: 6-44,** 4-Y-O: 3-29, 5-Y-O: 1-8, 6-Y-O+: 0-3.
FAVOURITES\SECOND FAVOURITES (strike rate and to a £1 stake): Favs. 20 per cent, -£5.99, **S.Favs. 25 per cent, +£4.**
AVERAGE WINNING RATING: 120.

Introduction

This always attracts some of Europe's finest milers and has featured some outstanding battles, notably Marling's heart-stopping head victory over Selkirk in 1992.

Ten year analysis

Age: Three and four-year-olds are dominant, with the younger generation holding the call.

Weight/Rating: All the winners were rated between 118 and 124. As that indicates, this is a race for proven horses.

Form: Seven won beforehand (all over seven furlongs or a mile). However, it is more interesting to note that eight ran at Royal Ascot, two winning, five making the frame and one finishing unplaced.

Latest start: Eight completed their preparation in a Group One or Two contest, two winning and five finishing second. Avoid those taking a big step-up in class.

Best trial: The Queen Anne Stakes is the pick of the Royal Ascot's trials. Among Men, Distant Relative and Ali-Royal made the frame in that event, while Sayyedati was unplaced.

Betting: Favourites have a weak record, but second favourites have managed to produce a level-stakes profit.

Top trainers: There are no outstanding trends, although both Henry Cecil and Geoff Wragg have saddled a brace of winners.

GOODWOOD, WEDNESDAY AUGUST 2
*TOTE GOLD TROPHY HANDICAP (0-105) THREE-YEAR-OLDS (1m 4f)

YR	FORM	WINNER	WT	RATING	S.P.	DRAW	GOING	TRAINER	JOCKEY	FORM IN YEAR WN-RN	WN DIST.
93	30-1133	**DANA SPRINGS**	8.11	99	10-1	14	GD-SFT	R.Hannon	L.Dettori	2-4	8,12f
94	0-10312	**MIDNIGHT LEGEND**	9.07	94	9-2F	8	FM	L.Cumani	J.Weaver	2-5	8,12f
95	00-201	**PILSUDSKI**	8.12	89	11-2(SF)	14	FM	Sir M.Stoute	W.Swinburn	1-3	10f
96	-31100	**FREEQUENT**	8.09	90	9-1	4	GD-FM	L.Cumani	Pat Eddery	2-5	8,8.5f
97	21-U012	**MAYLANE**	9.04	99	13-2	15	GD-FM	A.Stewart	M.Roberts	1-4	9f
98	34-201	**MUHIB**	9.01	96	10-1	14	GD-SFT	Sir M.Stoute	R.Hills	1-3	9f
99	0-11	**MARY STUART**	8.09	87	9-4F	7	GD-FM	Sir M.Stoute	G.Stevens	2-2	10f

* NO RACE 1990-1992.

FAVOURITES\SECOND FAVOURITES (strike rate and to a £1 stake): **Favs. 29 per cent, +£1.75,** S.Favs. 11 per cent, -£2.50.
AVERAGE WINNING RATING: 93.
TOP TRAINER (wins-runners, strike rate and to a £1 stake): **Sir Michael Stoute (3-4, 75 per cent, +£16.75).**

Introduction

Restricted to three-year-olds since 1993, this is often the target of embryonic Group racers. Pilsudski is the pick of the seven winners to date, but Dana Springs, Midnight Legend and Maylane were also capable of mixing it with the big boys.

Ten year analysis

Weight/Rating: All the winners were rated between 87 and 99, none carrying less than 8st 9lbs. This is not a light-weights race.

Form: Only two scored as juveniles, hinting that this is best left to late-maturing types. However, all seven managed to win earlier in their year and maidens must be avoided.

Latest start: All seven ran in a handicap around ten furlongs from June on their latest start, two winning and three making the frame.

Best trial: The Duke Of Cambridge Handicap – a ten-furlong three-year-olds' event run at Newmarket's July Meeting – has been a sound pointer. Pilsudski won that heat, Maylane finished second and Freequent unplaced.

Betting: Favourites have shown a small profit, but the market is not an inspired guide.

Top trainers: Sir Michael Stoute has a superb record, sending out three winners from just four runners. That trend is too good to ignore and anything he sends here must be treated with huge respect.

GOODWOOD, WEDNESDAY AUGUST 2
RICHMOND STAKES (GROUP 2) TWO-YEAR-OLD COLTS AND GELDINGS (6f)

YR	FORM	WINNER	WT	S.P.	DRAW	GOING	TRAINER	JOCKEY	FORM IN YEAR WN-RN	FORM IN YEAR WN DIST.
90	211112	**MAC'S IMP**	8.11	2-1F	5	GD-FM	W.O'Gorman	A.Munro	4-6	5,6f
91	211	**DILUM**	8.11	2-7F	4	GD	P.Cole	A.Munro	2-3	6f
92	0111	**SON PARDO**	8.11	7-1	4	GD-FM	R,Hannon	J.Reid	3-4	6f
93	111	**FIRST TRUMP**	8.11	10-3(SF)	1	GD-SFT	G.Wragg	M.Hills	3-3	6f
94	2111	**SRI PEKAN**	8.11	9-4(SF)	6	FM	P.Cole	T.Quinn	3-4	5,6f
95	131	**POLARIS FLIGHT**	8.11	9-4(SF)	2	GD-FM	P.Chapple-Hyam	J.Reid	2-3	5,6f
96	11	**EASYCALL**	8.11	7-2(SF)	2	GD-FM	B.Meehan	B.Doyle	2-2	5f
97	1	**DAGGERS DRAWN**	8.11	8-13F	5	GD-FM	H.Cecil	K.Fallon	1-1	6f
98	12	**MUQTARIB**	8.11	9-2	4	GD-SFT	J.Dunlop	R.Hills	1-2	6f
99	1	**BACHIR**	8.11	11-8F	5	GD-FM	J.Gosden	L.Dettori	1-1	6f

FAVOURITES/SECOND FAVOURITES (strike rate and to a £1 stake): **Favs. 40 per cent, -£1.72, S.Favs. 40 per cent, +£5.33.**

Introduction

This is a desperate long-term guide - Mac's Imp, Dilum, Sri Pekan, First Trump, Easycall and Daggers Drawn all disappointed to varying degrees during their second season. Bear this damning evidence in mind when assessing the future of any Richmond Stakes winner.

Ten year analysis

Form: Only one made his debut before May, while nine won over six furlongs during their preparation. Six had run in a Group or Listed event, each winning. It is also worth noting that five scored at Newmarket.

Latest start: Eight of the last ten came here direct from a win, seven over six furlongs.

Best trial: Royal Ascot's Coventry Stakes is the pick of our trials - Dilum, Mac's Imp and Sri Pekan all won that event.

Betting: Favourites and second favourites have won eight of the ten runnings since 1990. This has been a good race for those who follow the market.

Top trainer: Paul Cole has a decent record, saddling two winners and two placed horses during the past decade.

GOODWOOD, THURSDAY AUGUST 3

LANSON CHAMPAGNE VINTAGE STAKES (GROUP 3) TWO-YEAR-OLDS (7f)

									FORM IN YEAR	
YR	FORM	WINNER	WT	S.P.	DRAW	GOING	TRAINER	JOCKEY	WN-RN	WN DIST.
90	1	MUKADDAMAH	8.11	6-4F	5	GD-FM	P.Walwyn	W.Carson	1-1	6f
91	121	DR DEVIOUS	9.00	9-4(SF)	5	GD	P.Chapple-Hyam	W.Carson	2-3	6,7f
92	12	MAROOF	8.11	8-1	5	GD-FM	R.Armstrong	W.Carson	1-2	5f
93	13	MISTER BAILEYS	8.11	13-8F	2	GD-SFT	M.Johnston	D.Mckeown	1-2	6f
94	21	ELTISH	8.11	8-11F	6	FM	H.Cecil	Pat Eddery	1-2	7f
95	1	ALHAARTH	8.11	5-6F	5	FM	W.Hern	W.Carson	1-1	7f
96	1	PUTRA	8.11	10-3(SF)	6	GD-FM	P.Cole	T.Quinn	1-1	7f
97	411	CENTRAL PARK	9.00	5-4F	1	GD-FM	P.Cole	Pat Eddery	2-3	6,7f
98	1	ALJABR	8.11	4-6F	2	GD-SFT	S.Bin Suroor	L.Dettori	1-1	7f
99	2	EKRAAR	8.11	7-4(SF)	5	GD-FM	M.Tregoning	R.Hills	0-1	

FAVOURITES\SECOND FAVOURITES (strike rate and tc a £1 stake): **Favs. 60 per cent, +£2.73, S.Favs. 30 per cent,** +£0.33.

Introduction

This numbers the Classic heroes Dr Devious and Mister Baileys among its recent winners and can be regarded as an above-average Group Three.

Ten year analysis

Weight/Rating: Only two of the last ten – Dr Devious and Central Park – carried a penalty

Form: None made their debut before May or ran more than three times beforehand.
Nine scored during their preparation – all from June - six over seven furlongs. Only one had run in a Group race.

Latest start: Seven won their most recent outing, six over seven furlongs. Indeed, it is important to note that eight had their latest start over that trip.

Betting: This has been an excellent race for favourites, 60 per cent winning since 1990. Second favourites show a profit during the same period and shock results are scarce.

Top trainer: Henry Cecil used to have an excellent record, but has not saddled a winner since Eltish in 1994. Paul Cole has struck twice since then and could be the man to watch.

GOODWOOD, THURSDAY AUGUST 3

GOODWOOD CUP (GROUP 2) (2m)

YR	FORM	WINNER	AGE-WT	RATING	S.P.	DRAW	GOING	TRAINER	JOCKEY	FORM IN YEAR WN-RN	WN DIST.
90	001111	**LUCKY MOON**	3 7.10	-	11-8F	6	GD-FM	J.Dunlop	W.Carson	4-6	12,14,16f
91	112-101	**FURTHER FLIGHT**	5 9.00	100	9-2	10	GD	B.Hills	M.Hills	2-3	12,15f
92	2011-00	**FURTHER FLIGHT**	6 9.05	114	7-1	9	GD-FM	B.Hills	M.Hills	0-2	
93	222-132	**SONUS**	4 9.03	116	4-1(SF)	7	GD-SFT	J.Gosden	Pat Eddery	1-3	11f
94	001-213	**TIOMAN ISLAND**	4 9.05	107	10-1	9	FM	P.Cole	T.Quinn	1-3	15f
95	10-1411	**DOUBLE TRIGGER**	4 9.05	117	2-1F	7	GD-FM	M.Johnston	J.Weaver	3-4	16,20f
96	211-240	**GREY SHOT**	4 9.00	110	3-1(SF)	4	GD-FM	I.Balding	Pat Eddery	0-3	
97	1210-00	**DOUBLE TRIGGER**	6 9.00	115	16-1	1	GD-FM	M.Johnston	M.Roberts	0-2	
98	140-002	**DOUBLE TRIGGER**	7 9.05	119	11-2(SF)	4	GD-SFT	M.Johnston	D.Holland	0-3	
99	1041-13	**KAYF TARA**	5 9.07	119	9-4JF	5	GD-FM	S.Bin Suroor	L.Dettori	1-2	15.5f

AGE (wins-runners): 3-Y-O: 1-18, 4-Y-O: 4-35, 5-Y-O: 2-21, **6-Y-O+: 3-19.**
FAVOURITES/SECOND FAVOURITES (strike rate and to a £1 stake): Favs. 25 per cent, -£2.38, **S.Favs. 25 per cent, +£3.50.**
AVERAGE WINNING RATING: 113.
TOP TRAINER (wins-runs, strike rate and to a £1 stake): **Mark Johnston (3-4, 75 per cent, +£22.50).**

Introduction

Like the Sussex Stakes, this race has featured some superb finishes over the past decade, the action usually revolving around Mark Johnston's chestnut warrior, Double Trigger.

Ten year analysis

Age: Those aged six and above have the best strike rate, while three-year-olds tend to struggle and have not scored since Lucky Moon in 1990.

Weight/Rating: Penalties are no anchor – the last two winners shouldered extra poundage.

Form: Eight had a maximum of three starts beforehand and your selection should not be over-raced.

Winning form is not essential (four failed to score), although it is worth noting that six made the frame up to 14 furlongs during their preparation. This indicates that a degree of speed can be helpful.

Latest start: The last five ran in a Group race on their latest start.

Best trials: Unsurprisingly, Royal Ascot's Gold Cup is an excellent trial. Four of the last ten ran in that marathon, Double Trigger winning in 1995, finishing second in 1998 and unplaced in 1997. Kayf Tara is the other Gold Cup graduate; he ran third there in 1999.

Our other leading trial is also staged at Ascot, namely the Sagaro Stakes (run in early May). Once again, four took part in that race, one winning, one finishing placed and two unplaced.

Betting: Second favourites have produced a slight profit since 1990, although Tioman Island (10/1) and Double Trigger (16/1) have both struck for the bookies.

Top trainer: Courtesy of the omnipresent Double Trigger, Mark Johnston has an excellent record in this event. His four runners since 1990 have yielded three wins and a second place.

GOODWOOD, THURSDAY AUGUST 3
WILLIAM HILL MILE HANDICAP (1m)

YR	FORM	WINNER	AGE-WT	RATING	S.P.	DRAW	GOING	TRAINER	JOCKEY	FORM IN YEAR WN-RN	WN DIST.
90	021/014	**MARCH BIRD**	5 7.08	73	15-1	15	GD-FM	J.Sutcliffe	N.Adams	1-3	8f
91	10-2140	**SKY CLOUD**	5 8.07	85	20-1	13	GD	R.Akehurst	T.Quinn	1-4	7f
92	-2101	**LITTLE BEAN**	3 8.02	84	9-1(SF)	8	GD-FM	G.Wragg	M.Hills	2-4	8f
93	40-0234	**PHILIDOR**	4 8.04	86	13-2(SF)	13	GD-SFT	J.Eustace	N.Kennedy	0-4	
94	01420-2	**FRAAM**	5 9.09	105	10-1	15	FM	A.Scott	W.Swinburn	0-1	
95	002102	**KHAYRAPOUR**	5 7.13	83	15-2(SF)	1	GD-FM	B.Meehan	B.Doyle	1-6	8f
96	022-004	**MOSCOW MIST**	5 7.10	75	66-1	16	GD-FM	Lady Herries	D.O'Shea	0-3	
97	120410	**FLY TO THE STARS**	3 9.06	106	14-1	19	GD-FM	M.Johnston	O.Peslier	2-6	8f
98	2-33101	**FOR YOUR EYES ONLY**	4 9.06	102	14-1	8	GD-SFT	T.D.Easterby	J.Weaver	2-5	8f
99	420-102	**LONESOME DUDE**	4 9.07	103	7-1(SF)	12	GD-FM	Sir M.Stoute	G.Stevens	1-3	8f

AGE (wins-runners): 3-Y-O: 2-55, 4-Y-O: 3-62, **5-Y-O: 5-45,** 6-Y-O+: 0-29.
FAVOURITES/SECOND FAVOURITES (strike rate and to a £1 stake): Favs. 0 per cent, -£10, **S.Favs. 36 per cent, +£23.**
AVERAGE WINNING RATING: 90.

Introduction

First run in 1987, this has become a popular port of call for Group-class milers - the recent winners include Waajib, Safawan, Fraam and Fly To The Stars. Their successor is worth following if he steps up in class.

Ten year analysis

Age: No horse aged above five has won. This is not one for the 'wrinklies'.

Weight/Rating: Winners have come from all sections of the weights and ratings.

Draw: High numbers are preferred - only one of the last ten was drawn lower than eight.

Form: Seven had a maximum of four starts beforehand, the same number winning a seven-furlong or mile handicap from May.

Latest start: Seven ran in a handicap over seven furlongs or a mile from June on their latest start, two winning and four making the frame.

Best trial: Four completed their preparation in the valuable mile handicap run on Sandown's Eclipse Stakes card, For Your Eyes Only winning, while March Bird, Khayrapour and Lonesome Dude made the frame.

Betting: Favourites have drawn a blank since this race's inception, although second favourites have produced excellent returns.

GOODWOOD, FRIDAY AUGUST 4
VOLVO CONTRACTS GLOBETROTTER HANDICAP (0-110) THREE-YEAR-OLDS (1m 2f)

YR	FORM	WINNER	WT	RATING	S.P.	DRAW	GOING	TRAINER	JOCKEY	FORM IN YEAR WN-RN	WN DIST.
90	401022	**KAWTUBAN**	9.02	88	7-1	6	FM	R.Charlton	W.Carson	1-7	8f
91	0-1	**GREEN DANUBE**	8.02	82	25-1	7	GD	Ld Huntingdon	A.Munro	1-1	7.5f
92	30-4011	**PARTY CITED**	9.04	101	12-1	14	GD-FM	D.Elsworth	J.Williams	2-4	8,10f
93	4-410	**WESTERN CAPE**	8.12	92	14-1	18	GD-SFT	R.Charlton	Pat Eddery	1-3	8f
94	00-0111	**FRUSTRATION**	8.06	88	5-1(SF)	10	FM	Lady Herries	D.Harrison	3-4	10f
95	-2123	**JALFREZI**	7.10	84	6-1(SF)	6	GD-FM	J.Toller	S.Sanders	1-4	8f
96	0-11	**FAHIM**	8.13	94	5-2F	14	GD-FM	A.Stewart	R.Hills	2-2	8f
97	1-10202	**FUTURE PERFECT**	8.09	88	25-1	1	GD-FM	P.Cole	C.Rutter	1-5	8f
98	01-3244	**GYPSY PASSION**	8.10	91	6-1	2	GD-SFT	M.Johnston	O.Peslier	0-4	
99	0-14	**AZOUZ PASHA**	8.09	96	9-1	11	GD-FM	H.Cecil	K.Fallon	1-2	10f

FAVOURITES/SECOND FAVOURITES (strike rate and to a £1 stake): Favs. 9 per cent, -£7.50, **S.Favs. 12 per cent, -£3.**
A VERAGE WINNING RATING: 90.

Introduction

Formerly known as the 'Extel', this race is not quite as competitive as when won by Crimson Beau, Free Guest and Broken Hearted. That said, it remains a cracking heat.

Ten year analysis

Weight/Rating: This is not a race for those at either extreme of the handicap. The last four carried between 8st 9lbs and 8st 13lbs, a pattern that may continue.

Draw: While low numbers are disliked, horses drawn one and two have scored in the past three seasons.

Form: This is a race for late developers. Only two managed to score as juveniles, nine improving to win earlier in their year. Seven had a two-four start preparation, underlining that your selection should not have revealed everything to the Handicapper.

Latest start: Only one finished unplaced on his most recent outing, six running in a ten-furlong handicap.

Betting: This race has featured several spectacular gambles, but the market has been a poor guide recently.

Top trainers: Roger Charlton has sent out two decent-priced winners and a placed horse since 1990. His runners are worth a second glance. It is also worth pointing out that Luca Cumani used to have a superb record, Free Guest, Fish 'N Chips and Chinoiserie providing him with a hat-trick in the mid-eighties. The Newmarket-handler has cut little ice since then, but remains a man to watch closely.

GOODWOOD, SATURDAY AUGUST 5
NASSAU STAKES (GROUP 1) FILLIES AND MARES (1m 2f)

YR	FORM	WINNER	AGE-WT	RATING	S.P.	DRAW	GOING	TRAINER	JOCKEY	FORM IN YEAR WN-RN	WN DIST.
90	-110	**KARTAJANA**	3 8.06	-	11-2	3	FM	Sir M.Stoute	W.Swinburn	2-3	10f
91	11-3011	**RUBY TIGER**	4 9.04	-	11-4(SF)	2	GD-FM	P.Cole	T.Quinn	2-4	10,11f
92	0111-32	**RUBY TIGER**	5 9.01	121	2-1(SF)	4	GD-FM	P.Cole	T.Quinn	0-2	

93	-2111	**LYPHARD'S DELTA**	3 8.06	88	10-1	4	GD-SFT	H.Cecil	W.Ryan	3-4	8,10f
94	10-3132	**HAWAJISS**	3 8.06	115	4-1JF	4	FM	Sir M.Stoute	W.Swinburn	1-4	10f
95	3-201	**CARAMBA**	3 8.09	-	5-2F	3	GD-FM	R.Hannon	M.Roberts	1-3	8f
96	11-2	**LAST SECOND**	3 8.06	-	7-4F	1	GD-FM	Sir M.Prescott	G.Duffield	0-1	
97	121-441	**RYAFAN**	3 8.09	113	9-4F	5	GD-FM	J.Gosden	M.Hills	1-3	8f
98	3311-1	**ALBORADA**	3 8.09	107	4-1(SF)	5	GD	Sir M.Prescott	G.Duffield	1-1	10f
99	0-13	**ZAHRAT DUBAI**	3 8.06	115	5-1	3	FM	S.Bin Suroor	G.Stevens	1-2	10f

AGE (wins-runners): **3-Y-O: 8-50**, 4-Y-O: 1-22, 5-Y-O: 1-3. 6-Y-O+: 0-0..
FAVOURITES/SECOND FAVOURITES (strike rate and to a £1 stake): **Favs. 36 per cent,+£3.50,** S.Favs. 23 per cent, -£1.25.
AVERAGE WINNING RATING: 110.

Introduction

Granted Group One status last season, this race rarely falls to a champion and is usually won by a filly that failed in the Classics.

Ten year analysis

Age: Three-year-olds have won eight of the last ten runnings and are strongly favoured.

Form: None had more than four starts beforehand, eight winning a Group or Listed event. Five of the winning three-year-olds ran in a Classic during her preparation, three making the frame and two finishing unplaced.

Latest start: Nine ran in a Group one or Two event from June on their latest start, four winning and four making the frame.

Best trial: Three ran in the Epsom Oaks, Hawajiss and Zahrat Dubai finishing third, while Kartajana was unplaced.

Betting: Favourites have a useful strike rate and level-stakes profit. This is not a race for outsiders.

Top trainer: Sir Michael Stoute has sent out two winners during the period under study, Paul Cole bettering that with two winners and a placed horse. However, it may be more significant to note Sir Mark Prescott's two successes in the past four seasons. Sparing with his entries in this class, Newmarket's shrewdest operator must be respected if running anything here in the future.

GOODWOOD, SATURDAY AUGUST 5
STEWARDS' CUP HANDICAP (6f)

YR	FORM	WINNER	AGE-WT	RATING	S.P.	DRAW	GOING	TRAINER	JOCKEY	FORM IN YEAR WN-RN	WN DIST.
90	043411	**KNIGHT OF MERCY**	4 9.00	92	14-1	18	GD-FM	R.Hannon	B.Raymond	2-6	6,7f
91	1/0-0441	**NOTLEY**	4 8.12	95	14-1	28	GD	R.Hannon	R.Perham	1-4	5f
92	211-314	**LOCHSONG**	4 8.00	82	10-1	5	GD-FM	I.Balding	W.Carson	1-3	6f
93	11000-1	**KING'S SIGNET**	4 9.10	98	16-1	21	GD-SFT	J.Gosden	W.Carson	1-1	5f
94	0-30423	**FOR THE PRESENT**	4 8.03	81	16-1	16	FM	T.D.Barron	J.Fortune	0-5	
95	043020	**SHIKARI'S SON**	8 8.13	92	40-1	30	GD-FM	J.White	R.Hughes	1-8	6f
96	4231-01	**COASTAL BLUFF**	4 8.05	91	10-1JF	29	GD-FM	T.D.Barron	J.Fortune	1-2	5f
97	2-00021	**DANETIME**	3 8.10	100	5-1F	5	GD-FM	N.Callaghan	Pat Eddery	1-5	6f
98	200311	**SUPERIOR PREMIUM**	4 8.12	99	14-1	28	GD	R.Fahey	R.Winston	2-7	6f
99	024302	**HARMONIC WAY**	4 8.06	92	12-1	8	GD-FM	R.Charlton	R.Hughes	0-6	

AGE (wins-runners): 3-Y-O: 1-55, **4-Y-O: 8-92,** 5-Y-O: 0-55, 6-Y-O+: 1-88.
FAVOURITES/SECOND FAVOURITES (strike rate and to a £1 stake): **Favs. 14 per cent,** +£3, S.Favs. 0 per cent, -£12.
AVERAGE WINNING RATING: 92.

Introduction

Lochsong, Coastal Bluff, Danetime and Superior Finish went on from here to make their mark in Group events. Do not be surprised if their successor holds his own at a higher level.

Ten year analysis

Age: It is unusual for a major handicap to be dominated by one age group, but four-year-olds have a tremendous record, winning eight of the last ten runnings.

Weight/Rating: Only one of the last ten carried above 9st, while eight were rated between 91 and 100.

Draw: While low numbers dominated last season, those drawn high have the best overall record. Seven of the last ten came from stalls 16-30.

Form: Eight won earlier in their year, seven landing a five or six-furlong handicap from May.

Latest start: Your selection must come here with a good recent run over the trip to his name – four won and three were placed in a six-furlong handicap from June last time.

Best trial: Seven ran in Royal Ascot's Wokingham Handicap, Knight Of Mercy winning, Notley, Lochsong, Danetime and Superior Premium making the frame, while Shikari's Son and Coastal Bluff were unplaced.

Betting: Only one big outsider has won (Shikari's Son at 40/1) and this is usually best left to those in the 10/1 to 16/1 bracket.

Top trainers: Richard Hannon (two winners and two placed), David Barron (two winners) and Ian Balding (one winner and four placed) have noteworthy records.

NEWBURY, SATURDAY AUGUST 19
GEOFFREY FREER STAKES (GROUP 2) (1m 5f 61y)

YR	FORM	WINNER	AGE-WT	RATING	S.P.	DRAW	GOING	TRAINER	JOCKEY	FORM IN YEAR WN-RN	WN DIST.
90	133420	**CHARMER**	5 9.02	-	4-1	5	GD-FM	C.Brittain	L.Dettori	1-6	12f
91	14-0321	**DRUM TAPS**	5 9.05	-	15-2	5	GD-FM	Ld Huntingdon	L.Dettori	1-4	12f
92	0-23020	**SHAMBO**	5 9.03	107	9-1	4	GD	C.Brittain	M.Roberts	0-5	
93	1-14434	**AZZILFI**	3 8.05	110	5-1(SF)	4	GD-FM	J.Dunlop	W.Carson	1-5	10f
94	-22121	**RED ROUTE**	3 8.05	107	11-10F	5	GD	H.Cecil	W.Ryan	2-5	10,14f
95	113331	**PRESENTING**	3 8.05	119	10-11F	5	GD-FM	J.Gosden	J.Reid	3-6	10,12f
96	01-0020	**PHANTOM GOLD**	4 9.03	111	6-1	5	GD	Ld Huntingdon	L.Dettori	0-4	
97	120-200	**DUSHYANTOR**	4 9.06	120	9-2(SF)	5	GD-FM	H.Cecil	K.Fallon	0-3	
98	2/24-032	**MULTICOLOURED**	5 9.03	112	10-1	1	GD	Sir M.Stoute	W.Ryan	0-3	
99	221-144	**SILVER PATRIARCH**	5 9.09	121	7-2	1	GD	J.Dunlop	Pat Eddery	1-3	12f

AGE (wins-runners): 3-Y-O: 3-9, 4-Y-O: 2-21, **5-Y-O: 5-14,** 6-Y-O+: 0-11.
FAVOURITES/SECOND FAVOURITES (strike rate and to a £1 stake): Favs. 20 per cent, -£5.99, **S.Favs. 13 per cent, -£3.50.**
AVERAGE WINNING RATING: 113.

Introduction

Although three-year-olds have a fair record, this Group Two cannot be regarded as a good St Leger trial. No horse has won both races during the past 20 years.

Ten year analysis:

Age: Three and five-year-olds have the best strike rates, while none aged above six have managed to score during the past decade.

Weight/Rating: As an average win rating of 113 implies, this is not the hottest Group Two in the calendar.

Form: Six won during their preparation, five landing a Group or Listed contest.

Latest start: Nine had their latest start over 12 furlongs. This is best left to those stepping-up, rather than dropping back, in distance.

Betting: Favourites and second favourites have produced a level-stakes loss over the past decade. The market is a poor guide.

Top trainer: Clive Brittain is not usually a trainer to support blindly, but he has an excellent record in this event. The never-say-die Newmarket handler has sent out three winners from just six runners since 1988, producing a massive 30 point level-stakes profit.

YORK, TUESDAY AUGUST 22
JUDDMONTE INTERNATIONAL STAKES (GROUP 1) (1m 2f 85y)

YR	FORM	WINNER	AGE-WT	RATING	S.P.	DRAW	GOING	TRAINER	JOCKEY	FORM IN YEAR WN-RN	WN DIST.
90	3-20114	**IN THE GROOVE**	3 8.09	-	4-1	3	GD	D.Elsworth	S.Cauthen	2-5	8,10f
91	0-12304	**TERIMON**	5 9.06	119	16-1	6	GD	C.Brittain	M.Roberts	1-5	9f
92	1-41104	**RODRIGO DE TRIANO**	3 8.12	-	8-1	12	GD	P.Chapple-Hyam	L.Piggott	2-5	8f
93	230-120	**EZZOUD**	4 9.06	115	28-1	3	GD-SFT	Sir M.Stoute	W.Swinburn	1-3	9f
94	0-0321U	**EZZOUD**	5 9.06	120	4-1	4	GD-FM	Sir M.Stoute	W.Swinburn	1-5	10f
95	111-111	**HALLING**	4 9.06	120	9-4F	2	GD-FM	S.Bin Suroor	W.Swinburn	3-3	8,10f
96	10-1011	**HALLING**	5 9.05	128	6-4F	1	GD	S.Bin Suroor	L.Dettori	3-4	9.10f
97	121-114	**SINGSPIEL**	5 9.05	128	4-1(SF)	2	GD	Sir M.Stoute	L.Dettori	2-3	10,12f
98	1/11-01	**ONE SO WONDERFUL**	4 9.02	116	6-1	5	GD-FM	L.Cumani	Pat Eddery	1-2	10f
99	1310-22	**ROYAL ANTHEM**	4 9.05	125	3-1JF	9	GD	H.Cecil	G.Stevens	0-2	

AGE (wins-runners): 3-Y-O: 2-37, 4-Y-O: 4-28, **5-Y-O: 4-15**, 6-Y-O+: 0-2.
FAVOURITES/SECOND FAVOURITES (strike rate and to a £1 stake): **Favs. 27 per cent, -£1.25,** S.Favs. 10 per cent, -£5.
AVERAGE WINING RATING: 121.
TOP TRAINER (wins-runners, strike rate and to a £1 stake): **Sir Michael Stoute (3-9, 33 per cent, +£30).**

Introduction

Love him or loath him, Royal Anthem put up a superlative display when winning this race last term. Indeed, with Halling, Singspiel and Rodrigo de Triano being equally impressive, this is an event to savour.

Ten year analysis

Age: Five-year-olds have an excellent record, furthering the case for keeping top-class horses in training.

Weight/Rating: An average win rating of 121 says plenty about this race. Only Premier League runners need apply.

Form: To underline the fact that this is a race for proven horses, eight landed a Group contest beforehand, six winning and two finishing placed in a Group One.

Latest start: Seven completed their preparation in a Group One, two winning, four making the frame and the hapless Ezzoud unseating.

Best trial: Four ran in the Coral-Eclipse Stakes at Sandown, Ezzoud (in 1994) and Halling (in 1995 and 1996) winning, while Terimon finished unplaced.

Betting: There have been plenty of shock results over the years. However, punters have had some respite in recent seasons, favourites winning three of the past five renewals.

Top trainer: Sir Michael Stoute has an excellent record, his nine runners since 1990 resulting in three winners and three placed horses. That equates to a mouth-watering 30 point level-stakes profit.

YORK, TUESDAY AUGUST 22
GREAT VOLTIGEUR STAKES (GROUP 2) THREE-YEAR-OLD COLTS AND GELDINGS (1m 4f)

YR	FORM	WINNER	WT	RATING	S.P.	DRAW	GOING	TRAINER	JOCKEY	FORM IN YEAR WN-RN	WN DIST.
90	1-1131	**BELMEZ**	9.00	-	1-2F	2	GD	H.Cecil	S.Cauthen	3-4	11,12f
91	0-11002	**CORRUPT**	8.09	-	5-1	7	GD	N.Callaghan	Pat Eddery	2-5	8,12f
92	1-03021	**BONNY SCOT**	8.09	-	11-8F	1	GD	L.Cumani	L.Dettori	1-5	12f
93	0411-10	**BOB'S RETURN**	8.09	108	16-1	4	GD-SFT	M.Tompkins	P.Robinson	1-2	12f
94	-4111	**SACRAMENT**	8.09	108	6-1	6	GD-FM	Sir M.Stoute	W.Swinburn	3-4	8,10,12f
95	0-11112	**PENTIRE**	8.12	120	4-5F	1	GD-FM	G.Wragg	M.Hills	4-5	10,12f
96	1-1224	**DUSHYANTOR**	8.09	120	3-1(SF)	2	GD	H.Cecil	Pat Eddery	1-4	12f
97	1-21	**STOWAWAY**	8.09	-	6-5F	3	GD	S.Bin Suroor	L.Dettori	1-2	12f
98	4-211	**SEA WAVE**	8.09	111	7-2	2	GD-FM	S.Bin Suroor	L.Dettori	2-3	10,12f
99	13-1423	**FANTASTIC LIGHT**	8.09	120	4-1(SF)	6	GD	Sir M.Stoute	G.Stevens	1-4	10f

FAVOURITES/SECOND FAVOURITES (strike rate and to a £1 stake): **Favs. 40 per cent, -£2.13,** S.Favs. 17 per cent, -£3.
AVERAGE WINNING RATING: 114.

Introduction

This is a fair St Leger trial. Bob's Return went on to win our oldest Classic, while Sheriff's Star, Bonny Scot and Dushyantor made the frame at Doncaster.

Ten year analysis

Weight/Rating: Only two of the last ten carried the three or five pound penalty incurred a previous win in Group One or Two company.

Form: Eight won as two-year-olds, while all ten scored earlier in their year, seven in Group races from 10-12 furlongs.
It is worth noting that six ran in a Group One during their preparation, although only four took part in a Classic.

Latest start: Eight ran in a Group race on their latest start, three winning and four making the frame.

Betting: Favourites boast a useful strike rate (40 per cent) but, like second favourites, yield a level-stakes loss.

Top trainers: Henry Cecil, Sir Michael Stoute and Saeed Bin Suroor have carved this race up over the past decade, each saddling two winners.

YORK, WEDNESDAY AUGUST 23
YORKSHIRE OAKS (GROUP 1) FILLIES AND MARES (1m 4f)

YR	FORM	WINNER	AGE-WT	RATING	S.P.	DRAW	GOING	TRAINER	JOCKEY	FORM IN YEAR WN-RN	WN DIST.
*90	4-11	**HELLENIC**	3 9.00	-	10-3(SF)	3	GD	Sir M.Stoute	W.Carson	2-2	10,12f
91	-03102	**MAGNIFICENT STAR**	3 8.11	-	16-1	1	GD	M.Moubarak	A.Cruz	1-5	10f
92	-1111	**USER FRIENDLY**	3 8.11	-	8-11F	3	GD-FM	C.Brittain	G.Duffield	4-4	10,12f
93	121-22	**ONLY ROYALE**	4 9.07	106	10-1	7	GD-SFT	L.Cumani	R.Cochrane	0-2	
94	1104-00	**ONLY ROYALE**	5 9.07	114	15-2	5	GD-FM	L.Cumani	L.Dettori	0-2	
95	314-131	**PURE GRAIN**	3 8.08	118	11-10F	2	GD-FM	Sir M.Stoute	J.Reid	2-3	10,12f
96	41-1123	**KEY CHANGE**	3 8.08	-	7-1	1	GD	J.Oxx(IR)	J.Murtagh	2-4	10f
97	0/0131-3	**MY EMMA**	4 9.04	113	7-1(SF)	7	GD	R.Guest	D.Holland	0-1	
98	-111	**CATCHASCATCHCAN**	3 8.08	107	2-1F	7	GD-FM	H.Cecil	K.Fallon	3-3	12f
99	32-1111	**RAMRUMA**	3 8.08	119	5-6F	9	GD	H.Cecil	Pat Eddery	4-4	12f

*THREE-YEAR-OLDS ONLY.

AGE (wins-runners): 3-Y-O: 6-53, **4-Y-O: 2-16,** 5-Y-O: 1-3, 6-Y-O+: 0-0.
FAVOURITES/SECOND FAVOURITES (strike rate and to a £1 stake): **Favs. 40 per cent, -£1.34,** S.Favs. 12 per cent, -£4.67.
AVERAGE WINNING RATING: 113.

Introduction

Like the Great Voltigeur, this is a decent St Leger trial. User Friendly won both events, while Hellenic, Roseate Tern and Ramruma made the frame on Town Moor after scoring here.

Ten year analysis

Age: Three-year-olds have had the best of the argument since this race was opened-up in 1991. However, older runners boast a superior strike rate and must not be dismissed lightly.

Weight/Rating: An average win rating of 113 is disappointing for a Group One event.

Form: All the three-year-old winners scored earlier in their year, while none of the successful older runners managed that. Remember this clear demarcation point when making your selection.
It is also interesting to note that five of the three-year-old winners failed to score as juveniles.

Latest start: Eight completed their preparation in a Group One or Two event, four winning and three making the frame.

Best trial: The Epsom and Irish Oaks' are our most reliable trials. Three fillies ran in both races, User Friendly and Ramruma completing the double, while Pure Grain finished third at Epsom before winning on The Curragh.

Betting: This has not been a great race for market leaders, favourites and second favourites producing a level-stakes loss.

Top trainers: Sir Michael Stoute has an excellent record, saddling two winners and six placed fillies since 1990.
Henry Cecil and Luca Cumani (two winners and two placed each) are other handlers to watch closely.

YORK, WEDNESDAY AUGUST 23
TOTE EBOR HANDICAP (1m 6f)

YR	FORM	WINNER	AGE-WT	RATING	S.P.	DRAW	GOING	TRAINER	JOCKEY	FORM IN YEAR WN-RN	WN DIST.
90	0-11021	**FURTHER FLIGHT**	4 8.08	80	7-1JF	3	GD	B.Hills	M.Hills	3-5	11,12,15f
91	011114	**DEPOSKI**	3 7.03	87	12-1	8	GD	Sir M.Stoute	F.Norton	4-6	12,13f
92	220210	**QUICK RANSOM**	4 8.03	81	16-1	1	GD-FM	M.Johnston	D.McKeown	2-8	12f
93	31-0400	**SARAWAT**	5 8.02	76	14-1	9	GD-SFT	R.Akehurst	T.Quinn	0-4	
94	2124-22	**HASTEN TO ADD**	4 9.03	92	13-2F	9	GD-FM	Sir M.Prescott	G.Duffield	0-2	
95	-4210	**SANMARTINO**	3 7.11	91	8-1	21	GD-FM	B.Hills	W.Carson	1-4	12f
96	4-23201	**CLERKENWELL**	3 7.11	98	17-2	2	GD	SirM.Stoute	F.Lynch	1-5	14f
97	001002	**FAR AHEAD**	5 8.00	82	33-1	10	GD	J.L.Eyre	T.Williams	1-6	12f
98	2-2132	**TUNING**	3 8.07	102	9-2F	1	GD-FM	H.Cecil	K.Fallon	1-4	14f
99	4210-12	**VICIOUS CIRCLE**	5 8.04	90	11-1	7	GD	L.Cumani	K.Darley	1-2	10f

AGE (wins-runners): **3-Y-O: 4-32,** 4-Y-O: 3-102, 5-Y-O: 3-40, 6-Y-O+: 0-39.
FAVOURITES/SECOND FAVOURITES (strike rate and to a £1 stake): F**avs. 23 per cent, +£8,** S.Favs. 0 per cent, -£18.
AVERAGE WINNING RATING: 88.

Introduction

The Ebor is often won by a horse capable of holding his own in Group or Listed company. Further Flight, Quick Ransom, Tuning and Vicious Circle fall into that category and your selection must have a touch of class.

Ten year analysis

Age: Three-year-olds have the best strike rate, while no horse aged above five has won in the past decade.

Weight/Rating: This is not a race for high-weights – none of the last ten carried more than 8st 8lbs.

Draw: Low draws are preferred – nine came from stalls one-ten.

Form: Eight won during their preparation, six from 12-14 furlongs. It is also worth noting that five had a maximum of four outings beforehand.

Latest start: Eight completed their preparation in a handicap, one winning and four making the frame.

Betting: Far Ahead (33/1) is the only total outsider to have scored during the last decade, and favourites have produced a healthy level-stakes profit.

Top trainer: Sir Michael Stoute has laid out a couple of smart three-year-olds - Deposki and Clerkenwell – to win this race. Keep a close eye on anything he runs in the future.

YORK, WEDNESDAY AUGUST 23
GIMCRACK STAKES (GROUP 2) TWO-YEAR-OLD COLTS AND GELDINGS (6f)

YR	FORM	WINNER	WT	S.P.	DRAW	GOING	TRAINER	JOCKEY	FORM IN YEAR WN-RN	WN DIST.
90	11	**MUJTAHID**	9.03	1-2F	4	GD	R.Armstrong	W.Carson	2-2	6f
91	212	**RIVER FALLS**	9.00	9-4(SF)	5	GD	R.Hannon	B.Raymond	1-3	6f
92	3110	**SPLENDENT**	9.00	8-1	1	GD-FM	P.Cole	A.Munro	2-4	6f
93	11431	**TURTLE ISLAND**	9.05	5-2(SF)	3	GD-SFT	P.Chapple-Hyam	J.Reid	3-5	5,6f
94	034	**CHILLY BILLY**	9.00	12-1	10	GD-FM	L.Ramsden	K.Fallon	0-3	

95	11	**ROYAL APPLAUSE**	9.00	4-6F	1	GD-FM	B.Hills	W.Swinburn	2-2	5,6f
96	12	**ABOU ZOUZ**	8.11	4-1	7	GD	D.Loder	L.Dettori	1-2	5f
97	14	**CARROWKEEL**	8.11	16-1	1	GD	B.Hills	Pat Eddery	1-2	5f
98	3	**JOSR ALGARHOUD**	8.11	6-1	7	GD-FM	M.Channon	K.Fallon	0-1	
99	12	**MULL OF KINTYRE**	8.11	5-6F	7	GD	A.O'Brien(IR)	M.Kinane	1-2	6f

FAVOURITES/SECOND FAVOURITES (strike rate and to a £1 stake): Favs. 25 per cent, -£7.01, **S.Favs. 20 per cent, -£3.25.**

Introduction

While Turtle Island went on to win a Classic, most recent Gimcrack winners have proved somewhat disappointing as three-year-olds. This is not a great long-term guide.

Ten year analysis

Weight/Rating: Mujtahid, Turtle Island and Royal Applause all scored while carrying a penalty. Extra poundage is no bar to success.

Form: Eight won beforehand, six over six furlongs. Five had run in Group races, three winning and one finishing second. Avoid any that failed to shine when tried in this grade.

Latest start: Nine ran over six furlongs on their latest start, three winning and five making the frame.

Best trial: There are no outstanding trials, although three did run in Newmarket's Group Three July Stakes, Mujtahid winning while Turtle Island and Mull Of Kintyre made the frame.

Betting: For a Group race that usually attracts a small field, this has been a poor race for favourite backers. Do not be afraid to look beyond the market leader.

Top trainer: No trainer has a stand-out record, although it is worth noting that Mick Channon has saddled a winner and second over the past two seasons.

YORK, THURSDAY AUGUST 24
LOWTHER STAKES (GROUP 2) TWO-YEAR-OLD FILLIES (6f)

YR	FORM	WINNER	WT	RATING	S.P.	DRAW	GOING	TRAINER	JOCKEY	FORM IN YEAR WN-RN	WN DIST.
90	312	**ONLY YOURS**	8.11	-	8-1	6	GD-FM	R.Hannon	B.Raymond	1-3	6f
91	12	**CULTURE VULTURE**	8.11	-	85-40(SF)	2	GD	P.Cole	T.Quinn	1-2	6f
92	11143	**NICHE**	9.00	-	2-1(SF)	4	GD-FM	R.Hannon	L.Piggott	3-5	5f

93	141	**VELVET MOON**	8.11	100	10-1	4	GD	P.Cole	A.Munro	2-3	6f
94	12	**HARAYIR**	8.11	-	2-1JF	6	GD-FM	W.Hern	W.Carson	1-2	6f
95	222	**DANCE SEQUENCE**	8.11	100	5-4F	8	GD-FM	Sir M.Stoute	W.Swinburn	0-3	
96	1	**BIANCA NERA**	8.11	-	6-1	6	GD-FM	D.Loder	K.Darley	1-1	5f
97	12	**CAPE VERDI**	8.11	-	7-4F	10	GD	P.Chapple-Hyam	J.Reid	1-2	6f
98	211	**BINT ALLAYL**	9.00	100	15-8F	1	FM	M.Channon	M.Kinane	2-3	5f
99	02121	**JEMIMA**	8.11	93	12-1	6	GD	T.D.Easterby	L.Charnock	2-5	5,6f

FAVOURITES/SECOND FAVOURITES (strike rate and to a £1 stake): **Favs 36 per cent, -£0.13**, S.Favs. 18 per cent, -£4.87.

Introduction

This must be regarded as a decent long-term guide. Harayir and Cape Verdi went on to land the 1000 Guineas, while Niche finished an honourable second in that event.

Ten year analysis

Weight/Rating: Only Niche and Bint Allayl have successfully carried a penalty since 1990.

Form: Nine won beforehand, seven from June. It is worth noting that six ran at Royal Ascot, where two won and three made the frame.

Latest start: Avoid any coming here on the back of a below-par performance – four won and six made the frame on their latest start.
Six completed their preparation in a Group race, one winning while, significantly, five made the frame.

Best trial: Royal Ascot's Queen Mary Stakes is our best trial. Four ran in that Group Three event, Bint Allayl winning, while Culture Vulture, Velvet Moon and Dance Sequence made the frame.

Betting: Four favourites have won since 1990 but, like second favourites, they still show a level-stakes loss.

Top trainer: There are no outstanding trainer trends, although Richard Hannon's two winners and two placed deserves a mention.

YORK, THURSDAY AUGUST 24
NUNTHORPE STAKES (GROUP 1) (5f)

YR	FORM	WINNER	AGE-WT	RATING	S.P.	DRAW	GOING	TRAINER	JOCKEY	FORM IN YEAR WN-RN	WN DIST.
90	2-01211	**DAYJUR**	3 9.03	-	8-11F	6	GD-FM	W.Hern	W.Carson	3-5	5,6f

91	0-1214	**SHEIKH ALBADOU**	3 9.03	-	6-1	3	GD	A.Scott	Pat Eddery	2-4	6f
92	1111	**LYRIC FANTASY**	2 7.08	-	8-11F	10	GD-FM	R.Hannon	M.Roberts	4-4	5f
93	344311	**LOCHSONG**	5 9.03	111	10-1	5	GD	I.Balding	L.Dettori	2-6	5f
*94	020102	**PICCOLO**	3 9.03	111	14-1	4	GD-FM	M.Channon	J.Reid	1-7	6f
95	112-210	**SO FACTUAL**	5 9.06	115	9-2	5	GD-FM	S.Bin Suroor	L.Dettori	1-3	6f
96	011-10	**PIVOTAL**	3 9.07	120	100-30	5	GD-FM	Sir M.Prescott	G.Duffield	1-2	5f
**97	010140	**YA MALAK**	6 9.09	116	11-1	4	GD	D.Nicholls	A.Greaves	3-8	5f
**97	111-010	**COASTAL BLUFF**	5 9.09	110	6-1(SF)	6	GD	T.D.Barron	K.Darley	1-3	5f
98	0-21223	**LOCHANGEL**	4 9.06	109	6-1	2	FM	I.Balding	L.Dettori	1-5	5.5f
99	123-241	**STRAVINSKY**	3 9.07	113	EV F	13	GD	A.O'Brien	M.Kinane	1-3	6f

* BLUE SIREN, 3 9.00, 14-1, I.Balding, M.Hills, finished first, disqualified and placed second.

** Dead-heat.

AGE (wins-runners): 2-Y-O: 1-4, **3-Y-O: 5-34,** 4-Y-O: 1-25, 5-Y-O: 3-26, 6-Y-O+: 1-25.

FAVOURITES/SECOND FAVOURITES (strike rate and to a £1 stake): Favs 30 per cent, -£4.16, **S.Favs. 9 per cent, -£4.**

AVERAGE WINNING RATING: 113.

Introduction

Our premier five-furlong dash, this has featured some fine finishes. Perhaps the pick of these came in 1997, when Coastal Bluff – whose bit broke soon after the start – managed to force a dead-heat with Ya Malak.

Ten year analysis

Age: Three-year-olds have the best strike rate, although winners have come from all divisions, including the juveniles.

Weight/Rating: The last eight were rated between 109 and 120. This is not a race for unproven horses.

Form: All 11 (including the dead-heaters) scored beforehand, six landing a five or six-furlong Group race from June. Only two – Sheikh Albadou and Lochsong – failed to run at either Royal Ascot or Newmarket's July Meeting, five taking part at both fixtures. Finally, note that four of the five winning three-year-olds began their season over seven furlongs.

Latest start: Nine ran in a Group race from June on their latest start, three winning and three making the frame.

Best trials: Newmarket's July Cup is an excellent trial. Five ran in that Group One event, Stravinsky winning, while Piccolo, So Factual, Pivotal and Coastal Bluff were unplaced. The Temple Stakes (run at Sandown on May 29) is another fair pointer. Four ran there, Dayjur winning, Lochsong and Lochangel making the frame, while Ya Malak finished out of the money.

Betting: Favourites and second favourites have a moderate record, while recent winners have returned at 10/1, 11/1 and 14/1.

Top trainer: Ian Balding has saddled two winners and two placed horses since 1990. Indeed, that record would read even more impressively had Blue Siren not been disqualified after scoring in 1994.

GOODWOOD, SATURDAY AUGUST 26
CELEBRATION MILE (GROUP 2) (1m)

YR	FORM	WINNER	AGE-WT	RATING	S.P.	DRAW	GOING	TRAINER	JOCKEY	FORM IN YEAR WN-RN	WN DIST.
90	21-3413	**SHAVIAN**	3 9.00	-	5-2F	1	GD-FM	H.Cecil	S.Cauthen	1-4	8f
91	2-42021	**BOLD RUSSIAN**	4 9.00	114	100-30	3	GD	B.Hills	W.Carson	1-5	7f
92	411-102	**SELKIRK**	4 9.03	128	1-2F	1	GD-SFT	I.Balding	R.Cochrane	1-3	8f
93	110423	**SWING LOW**	4 9.03	116	10-1	5	GD-FM	R.Hannon	J.Reid	2-7	7,8f
94	3-14130	**MEHTHAAF**	3 8.11	114	5-2(SF)	2	GD	J.Dunlop	W.Carson	2-5	7,8f
95	210331	**HARAYIR**	3 8.12	118	5-4F	3	FM	W.Hern	W.Carson	2-6	7,8f
96	21-10	**MARK OF ESTEEM**	3 9.01	120	11-4F	7	GD	S.Bin Suroor	L.Dettori	1-2	8f
*97	-1114	**AMONG MEN**	3 8.09	113	8-11F	2	GD-FM	Sir M.Stoute	M.Kinane	3-4	7,8f
98	20-3211	**MUHTATHIR**	3 8.09	119	11-4F	7	GD-FM	J.Gosden	R.Hills	2-4	7m8f
99	0340-31	**CAPE CROSS**	5 9.07	121	5-2(SF)	4	GD	S.Bin Suroor	J.Reid	1-2	8f

*CAPE CROSS, 3 8.09, 7-2, J.Gosden, L.Dettori, finished first, disqualified, placed fourth.

AGE (wins-runners): **3-Y-O: 6-34,** 4-Y-O: 3-19, 5-Y-O: 1-5, 6-Y-O+: 0-2.
FAVOURITES/SECOND FAVOURITES (strike rate and to a £1 stake): **Favs. 60 per cent, +£6.98,** S.Favs. 20 per cent, -£3.50.
AVERAGE WINNING RATING: 119

Introduction

While seldom as competitive as the Sussex Stakes, this race has witnessed some excellent performances, not least Mark Of Esteem's crushing victory in 1996.

Ten year analysis

Age: Three and four-year-olds dominate – only one aged five or above has scored since 1990.

Weight/Rating: As Selkirk, Swing Low, Mehthaaf, Harayir, Mark of Esteem and Cape Cross have demonstrated, penalties can be carried successfully.

Form: All ten won a Group race over seven furlongs or a mile beforehand. Avoid those who are unproven at this level.
Eight ran at Royal Ascot during their preparation, three winning, three making the frame and two finishing unplaced.

Latest start: Eight ran in a Group race from July on their latest start, three winning and four making the frame.

Best trial: There are no outstanding trials, although Newbury's Hungerford Stakes is a reasonable pointer.

Betting: Favourites boast an excellent 60 per cent strike rate and level-stakes profit.

Top trainer: Saeed Bin Suroor, who does particularly well with milers, has saddled two winners and two placed horses over the past five seasons. Expect him to improve that already smart record.

HAYDOCK, SATURDAY SEPTEMBER 2
STANLEY LEISURE SPRINT CUP (GROUP 1) (6f)

YR	FORM	WINNER	AGE-WT	RATING	S.P.	DRAW	GOING	TRAINER	JOCKEY	FORM IN YEAR WN-RN	WN DIST.
90	012111	**DAYJUR**	3 9.06	-	1-2F	7	GD	W.Hern	W.Carson	4-6	5,6f
91	22-1144	**POLAR FALCON**	4 9.09	-	13-2	4	GD-FM	J.Hammond(FR)	C.Asm'ssen	2-4	8f
92	221-134	**SHEIKH ALBADOU**	4 9.09	-	9-4JF	1	SFT	A.Scott	B.Raymond	1-3	5f
93	11-2242	**WOLFHOUND**	4 9.09	122	7-2	3	GD-FM	J.Gosden	M.Roberts	0-4	
94	11-4203	**LAVINIA FONTANA**	5 8.09	114	11-2	8	GD	J.Dunlop	J.Weaver	0-4	
95	34-3111	**CHEROKEE ROSE**	4 8.11	-	5-1(SF)	4	GD	J.Hammond(FR)	C.Asm'ssen	3-4	6.5,7f
96	200414	**IKTAMAL**	4 9.00	118	10-1	9	GD-FM	E.Dunlop	W.Ryan	2-9	6,7f
97	10-1112	**ROYAL APPLAUSE**	4 9.00	118	15-8F	9	GD-SFT	B.Hills	M.Hills	3-4	6f
98	112-012	**TAMARISK**	3 8.12	117	13-2	5	GD	R.Charlton	T.Sprake	1-3	6f
99	112-111	**DIKTAT**	4 9.00	119	13-8F	16	GD-FM	S.Bin Suroor	L.Dettori	3-3	6.5,7f

AGE (Wins-Runners): 3-Y-O: 2-44, **4-Y-O: 7-30,** 5-Y-O: 1-10, 6-Y-O+: 0-9.

FAVOURITES/SECOND FAVOURITES (Strike Rate and to £1 stake): Favs. 36 per cent, -£0.76, **S.Favs. 10 per cent, -£4.**

AVERAGE WINNING RATING: 118.

RACE RECORD: A genuine group 1, this has been won by crack sprinters like Dayjur, Sheikh Albadou, Royal Applause and Diktat.

Introduction

Granted Group One status in 1988, this race has gone on to attract some of Europe's finest sprinters. Recent winners include Dayjur, Sheikh Albadou, Royal Applause and Diktat, and your selection must be a class act.

Ten year analysis

Age: Four-year-olds have a wonderful record and are favoured.

Weight/Rating: None of the recent winners were rated below 114 - this is not a race for unproven horses.

Form: Eight won beforehand, seven landing a Group race. It is also worth noting that four won and two finished placed over seven furlongs or a mile during their preparation.

Latest start: Nine ran in a Group One or Two on their latest start, three winning and six making the frame.

Best trial: Six ran in Newmarket's July Cup, Polar Falcon, Sheikh Albadou, Iktamal, Royal Applause and Tamarisk making the frame, while Lavinia Fontana was unplaced.
The Prix Maurice de Gheest, a six and a half furlong event run at Deauville, is another useful pointer. Five of the ten ran there, Cherokee Rose and Diktat winning, while Wolfhound, Lavinia Fontana and Iktamal made the frame.

Betting: Favourites have a better record than second favourites, although the market has not been a great guide.

DONCASTER, WEDNESDAY SEPTEMBER 6
PORTLAND HANDICAP (0-110) (5f 140y)

YR	FORM IN YEAR FORM	WINNER	AGE-WT	RATING	S.P.	DRAW	GOING	TRAINER	JOCKEY	WN-RN	WN DIST.
90	010001	**LOVE LEGEND**	5 8.07	86	12-1	20	GD	D.Arbuthnot	A.Munro	5-13	5,6f
91	130112	**SARCITA**	3 8.06	85	13-2F	17	GD-FM	D.Elsworth	W.Carson	3-9	5,6f
92	11-3141	**LOCHSONG**	4 8.12	83	4-1F	16	GD	I.Balding	W.Carson	2-4	6f
93	100000	**AMRON**	6 9.00	86	12-1	9	GD-SFT	J.Berry	N.Carlisle	2-8	5,6f
94	000201	**HELLO MISTER**	3 8.10	97	12-1	3	GD	J.O'Donoghue	P.McCabe	4-15	5,6f
95	030403	**HELLO MISTER**	4 8.07	92	7-1F	3	GD-FM	J.O'Donoghue	P.McCabe	0-9	
96	020-000	**MUSICAL SEASON**	4 8.05	84	33-1	16	GD	T.D.Barron	K.Darley	0-3	
97	002133	**DASHING BLUE**	4 9.12	105	10-1	6	GD-FM	I.Balding	K.Darley	1-8	5f
98	011100	**CADEAUX CHER**	4 8.07	89	20-1	10	GD-FM	B.Hills	R.Cochrane	3-12	6f
99	130-201	**ASTONISHED**	3 9.06	99	11-2F	16	GD-FM	J,Hammond(FR)	K.Fallon	1-3	6f

AGE (Wins-Runners): 3-Y-O: 3-54, **4-Y-O: 5-62,** 5-Y-O: 1-32, 6-Y-O+: 1-63.

FAVOURITES/SECOND FAVOURITES (Strike rate and to £1 stake): **Favs.40 per cent, + £17**. S. Favs. 0 per cent, -£14.

AVERAGE WINNING RATING: 91.

Introduction

Run over the unusual five and a half furlong trip, this always attracts a hot field and has been won by Group-class sprinters Sarcita, Lochsong and Dashing Blue.

Ten year analysis

Age: Three and four-year-olds have dominated, with four-year-olds boasting a superior strike rate.

Weight/Rating: None of the last ten were rated below 84 or carried less than 8st 5lbs.

Draw: While winners have come from both sides of the track, high numbers may have a slight edge.

Form: Eight won over five or six furlongs beforehand, six landing a handicap over those trips from June.

Latest start: Nine completed their preparation in a five or six-furlong handicap, three winning and three making the frame.

Best trial: Goodwood's Stewards' Cup has been a fair trial. Four ran in that race, Lochsong winning, Dashing Blue making the frame, while Love Legend and Amron were unplaced.

Betting: Considering the size of field this race attracts, favourites have done well to produce a 40 per cent strike rate and 17 point level-stakes profit.

Top trainer: Ian Balding, who often has a couple of smart sprinters among his team, has sent out two winners and a placed horse since 1990.

DONCASTER, FRIDAY SEPTEMBER 8
CHAMPAGNE STAKES (GROUP 2) TWO-YEAR-OLD COLTS AND GELDINGS (7f)

YR	FORM	WINNER	WT	S.P.	DRAW	GOING	TRAINER	JOCKEY	FORM IN YEAR WN-RN	WN DIST
90	3	**BOG TROTTER**	8.11	8-1	1	GD	W.Haggas	N.Day	0-1	
91	111	**RODRIGO DE TRIANO**	8.11	11-8F	1	GD-FM	P.Chapple-Hyam	W.Carson	3-3	6,7f
92	110	**PETARDIA**	9.00	11-2(SF)	6	GD-FM	G.Wragg	M.Hills	2-3	5,6f
93	0112	**UNBLEST**	8.11	3-1(SF)	2	SFT	J.Fanshawe	G.Duffield	2-4	6f
94	21111	**SRI PEKAN**	9.00	10-3(SF)	3	GD	P.Cole	M.Kinane	4-5	5,6f
95	111	**ALHAARTH**	9.00	2-5F	1	GD-SFT	W.Hern	W.Carson	3-3	7f
96	11	**BAHHARE**	8.10	4-6F	3	GD-FM	J.Dunlop	W.Carson	2-2	7f
97	11	**DAGGERS DRAWN**	9.00	4-6F	4	GD-FM	H.Cecil	K.Fallon	2-2	6f

98	411	**AUCTION HOUSE**	8.10	7-2(SF)	8	GD	B.Hills	M.Hills	2-3	7f
99	1	**DISTANT MUSIC**	8.10	13-8F	1	GD-FM	B.Hills	M.Hills	1-1	7f

FAVOURITES/SECOND FAVOURITES (strike rate and to a £1 stake): Favs. 50 per cent -£0.29. **S. Favs. 33 per cent, +£7.33**

Introduction

This is an unreliable long-term guide. Petardia, Sri Pekan, Alhaarth, Bahhare, Daggers Drawn and Auction House all disappointed to varying degrees as three-year-olds.

Ten year analysis

Weight/Rating: Petardia, Sri Pekan, Alhaarth and Daggers Drawn have all carried penalties successfully since 1990.

Form: Only one made his debut before May - this is a not a race for early-season flying machines.
Nine won beforehand – eight from July onward - eight scoring at least twice.

Latest start: Seven won their latest start, five landing a Group or Listed event.

Betting: This is an excellent race for market leaders. Favourites and second favourites have won nine of the last ten renewals.

Top trainer: Barry Hills has won the last two runnings. Also responsible for three placed horses in the first half of the decade, he is obviously a trainer to watch closely.

DONCASTER, SATURDAY SEPTEMBER 9
ST LEGER STAKES (GROUP 1) THREE-YEAR-OLD COLTS AND FILLIES (1m 6f 132y)

YR	FORM IN YEAR FORM	WINNER	WT	RATING	S.P.	DRAW	GOING	TRAINER	JOCKEY	WN-RN	WN DIST.
90	321*-22	**SNURGE**	9.00	-	7-2	8	GD	P.Cole	T.Quinn	0-2	
91	1-3101	**TOULON**	9.00	-	5-2F	7	GD-FM	A.Fabre(FR)	Pat Eddery	2-4	12f
92	-11111	**USER FRIENDLY**	8.11	-	7-4F	2	GD-FM	C.Brittain	G.Duffield	5-5	10,12f
93	411-101	**BOB'S RETURN**	9.00	117	3-1F	9	SFT	M.Tompkins	P.Robinson	2-3	12f
94	112003	**MOONAX**	9.00	109	40-1	3	GD-SFT	B.Hills	Pat Eddery	2-6	10,12f
95	21-1420	**CLASSIC CLICHE**	9.00	118	100-30F	7	GD-SFT	S.Bin Suroor	L.Dettori	1-4	10f
96	213321	**SHANTOU**	9.00	115	8-1	10	GD-FM	J.Gosden	L.Dettori	2-7	10,11.5f

97	1-21202	**SILVER PATRIARCH**	9.00	123	5-4F	9	GD-FM	J.Dunlop	Pat Eddery	1-5	11.5f
98	-131	**NEDAWI**	9.00	113	5-2F	1	GD	S.Bin Suroor	L.Dettori	2-3	12f
99	21-1104	**MUTAFAWEQ**	9.00	116	11-2F	6	GD-FM	S.Bin Suroor	R.Hills	2-4	10,12f

* Disqualified.

FAVOURITES/SECOND FAVOURITES (strike rate and to a £1 stake): **Favs. 60 per cent, +£10.33,** S.Favs, 9 per cent, -£4.50.
AVERAGE WINNING RATING: 116.
TOP TRAINER (wins-runs, strike rate and to a £1 stake): **Saeed Bin Suroor (3-6, 50 per cent, +£8.33).**

Introduction

First run in 1776, our oldest Classic has enjoyed a renaissance in recent seasons. Snurge, Moonax, Classic Cliche, Shantou and Silver Patriarch were all kept in training to good effect, which bodes well for the long-term future of their successors.

Ten year analysis

Form: Nine won earlier in their year (eight scored at least twice), seven landing a Group race.
Eight ran in a 12-furlong Classic during their preparation, one winning, three making the frame and four finishing unplaced.

Latest start: Eight ran in a Group race over a mile and a half on their latest start, four winning and three making the frame.

Best trials: Four ran in the Epsom Derby, Shantou and Silver Patriarch making the frame while Toulon and Bob's Return were unplaced. Similarly, four ran in York's Great Voltigeur Stakes, Bob's Return winning, while Snurge, Silver Patriarch and Mutafaweq finished placed.

Betting: Favourites have a super record, recording a 60 per cent strike rate and £10.33 level-stakes profit.

Top trainer: Saeed Bin Suroor has an excellent record, sending out three winners and a placed horse from just six runners. That equates to a healthy level-stakes profit, and anything he runs here in the future must be treated with maximum respect.

DONCASTER, SATURDAY SEPTEMBER 9
FLYING CHILDERS STAKES (GROUP 2) TWO-YEAR-OLDS (5f)

YR	FORM	WINNER	WT	S.P.	DRAW	GOING	TRAINER	JOCKEY	FORM IN YEAR WN-RN	WN DIST.
90	14122	**DISTINCTLY NORTH**	8.11	6-4F	7	GD	J.Berry	Pat Eddery	2-5	5f
91	111212	**PARIS HOUSE**	8.11	4-6F	4	GD-FM	J.Berry	J.Carroll	5-7	5f
92	310	**POKER CHIP**	8.06	33-1	2	GD-FM	I.Balding	M.Hills	1-3	5f
93	141332	**IMPERIAL BAILIWICK**	8.06	12-1	5	GD-SFT	M.Usher	J.Williams	2-8	5
94	322114	**RAAH ALGHARB**	8.11	7-1	4	GD-SFT	M.Stoute	W.Swinburn	2-6	5,6f
95	123242	**CAYMAN KAI**	8.12	7-1	1	GD-SFT	R.Hannon	Pat Eddery	1-6	5f
96	1114	**EASYCALL**	9.03	5-1	1	GD-FM	B.Meehan	M.Tebbutt	3-4	5,6f
97	1202	**LAND OF DREAMS**	8.07	15-8F	5	GD-FM	M.Johnston	D.Holland	1-4	6f
98	13240	**SHEER VIKING**	8.12	9-1	2	GD	B.Hills	M.Hills	1-5	5f
99	222312	**MRS P**	8.07	33-1	13	GD-FM	L.Stubbs	Pat Eddery	1-7	5f

FAVOURITES/SECOND FAVOURITES (strike rate and to a £1 stake): **Favs. 27 per cent, -£3.97,** S.Favs. 0 per cent, -£11.

Introduction

This race is a poor long-term guide. Few recent winners proved capable of holding their own against the best older sprinters and their successors should be treated with a degree of caution.

Ten year analysis

Weight/Rating: Easycall is the only recent winner to defy a penalty. Stick with unpenalised entrants.

Form: All ten had run at least three times, each scoring over five or six furlongs. Seven ran in a Group race during their preparation, only one winning while five made the frame.

Latest start: Eight made the frame on their latest start, five in Group company. Look for horses that have shaped promisingly in this grade.

Best trial: Royal Ascot's five-furlong Group Three Norfolk Stakes is our best guide. Four ran there, Distinctly North, Paris House, Cayman Kai and Sheer Viking making the frame.

Betting: Favourites and second favourites have a poor record. With two recent winners being returned at 33/1, it could pay to look for some value.

LEOPARDSTOWN, SATURDAY SEPTEMBER 9
IRISH CHAMPION STAKES (GROUP 1) (1m 2f)

FORM IN YEAR

YR	FORM	WINNER	AGE-WT	S.P.	GOING	TRAINER	JOCKEY	WN-RN	WN DIST.
90	1022312	**ELMAAMUL**	3 8.11	2-1F	GD	W.Hern	W.Carson	2-6	8,10f
91	3-11212	**SUAVE DANCER**	3 8.11	4-6F	GD-SFT	J.Hammond(FR)	C.Asmussen	3-5	10,12f
92	1-20124	**DR DEVIOUS**	3 8.11	7-2(SF)	GD-SFT	P.Chapple-Hyam	J.Reid	1-5	12f
93	1/404-11	**MUHTARRAM**	4 9.04	7-1	GD	J.Gosden	W.Carson	2-2	8,9f
94	114121	**CEZANNE**	5 9.04	7-2(SF)	GD-SFT	Sir M.Stoute	M.Kinane	6-8	9,10,12f
95	111121	**PENTIRE**	3 8.11	9-4F	GD-FM	G.Wragg	M.Hills	5-6	10,12f
96	1-20211	**TIMARIDA**	4 9.01	3-1(SF)	GD	J.Oxx(IR)	J.Murtagh	2-5	9.5,10f
97	21-3212	**PILSUDSKI**	5 9.04	5-4F	GD	Sir M.Stoute	M.Kinane	1-4	10f
98	30-2231	**SWAIN**	6 9.04	6-4F	SFT	S.Bin Suroor	L.Dettori	1-4	12f
99	13-0211	**DAYLAMI**	5 9.04	6-4(SF)	SFT	s.Bin Suroor	L.Dettori	2-4	12f

AGE (wins-runners): 3-Y-O: 4-38, 4-Y-O: 2-25, **5-Y-O: 3-9**, 6-Y-O+: 1-5.
FAVOURITES/SECOND FAVOURITES (strike rate and to a £1 stake): Favs. 45 per cent, +£1.80. **S.Favs. 40 per cent, +£4.50.**

Introduction

This can lay claim to being Europe's premier ten-furlong event. The winners to date include outstanding horses like Suave Dancer, Dr Devious, Pentire, Pilsudski, Swain and Daylami.

Ten year analysis

Age: While three-year-olds provide most of the runners and winners, five-year-olds boast the best strike rate. Three winners from just nine runners since 1990 is an excellent return.

Form: Nine won a Group race during their preparation, seven landing a Group One. Seven showed top-class form over ten and 12 furlongs during their preparation. Look for a versatile horse when making your selection.

Latest start: Seven had their latest start in a Group One event, three winning and four making the frame.

Best trial: It is worth noting that the last three ran in Ascot's King George And Queen Elizabeth Diamond Stakes, Swain and Daylami winning, while Pilsudski finished second.

Best trial: This is an excellent race for favourite backers. First and second favourites have won nine of the last ten runnings, both producing a level-stakes profit.

Top trainer:	English raiders have won eight times since 1990. Saeed Bin Suroor and Sir Michael Stoute are the most successful handlers, producing two winners and two placed horses each.

AYR, SATURDAY SEPTEMBER 16
(AYR) GOLD CUP HANDICAP (6f)

YR	FORM	WINNER	AGE-WT	RATING	S.P.	DRAW	GOING	TRAINER	JOCKEY	FORM IN YEAR WN-RN	WN DIST.
90	221303	**FINAL SHOT**	3 8.02	81	12-1	8	GD-SFT	M.H.Easterby	J.Lowe	1-9	6f
91	301121	**SARCITA**	3 8.10	94	14-1	18	GD	D.Elsworth	B.Doyle	4-10	5,5.5,6f
92	1-31411	**LOCHSONG**	4 9.00	95	10-1(SF)	28	SFT	I.Balding	F.Arrowsmith	3-5	5.5,6f
93	000210	**HARD TO FIGURE**	7 9.06	101	12-1(SF)	8	GD-FM	R.Hodges	R.Cochrane	1-11	6f
94	310200	**DARING DESTINY**	3 8.00	89	18-1	29	GD-SFT	K.Burke	J.Tate	1-6	7f
95	103042	**ROYALE FIGURINE**	4 8.09	95	8-1	27	GD	M.F.Godley	D.Holland	1-6	5f
96	231-011	**COASTAL BLUFF**	4 9.10	104	3-1F	28	GD-FM	T.D.Barron	J.Fortune	2-3	5,6f
97	030001	**WILDWOOD FLOWER**	4 9.03	97	14-1	24	GD	R.Hannon	D.O'Neill	1-9	6f
98	000014	**ALWAYS ALIGHT**	4 8.07	89	16-1	8	GD-SFT	K.Burke	J.Egan	2-9	6f
99	021033	**GRANGEVILLE**	4 9.00	98	11-1(SF)	17	GD-SFT	I.Balding	K.Fallon	1-7	7f

AGE (wins- runners): 3-Y-O: 3-85, **4-Y-O: 6-86,** 5-Y-O: 0-46, 6-Y-O+: 1-69.
FAVOURITES/SECOND FAVOURITES (strike rate and to a £1 stake): Favs. 10 per cent, -£6. **S.Favs. 21 per cent, +£22.**
AVERAGE WINNING RATING: 94.

Introduction

Like the majority of handicaps in our guide, this is a first-class event. Lochsong and Coastal Bluff went on to win Group Ones, while Sarcita, Hard To Figure, Daring Destiny, Royal Figurine, Wildwood Flower and Grangeville were crack sprinters.

Ten year analysis

Age:	Three and four-year-olds have dominated, with four-year-olds boasting easily the best strike rate.
Weight/Rating:	There are no strong trends, Hard To Figure and Coastal Bluff both proving that big weights can be carried.
Draw:	There is always much discussion about the draw, recent evidence suggesting that high numbers have an edge. Seven of the last ten came from boxes 17-29.
Form:	All ten ran in a top-class handicap during their preparation, eight winning in that sphere over five or six furlongs.

Latest start: Seven ran in a five or six-furlong handicap from August on their latest start, four winning.

Best trial: Six ran in Royal Ascot's Wokingham Handicap, one making the frame and five finishing unplaced.

Betting: Only one favourite has scored and second favourites have a much better record, producing an excellent 22-point level-stakes profit.

Top trainers: Once again, Ian Balding comes to the fore in a sprint handicap, sending out two winners since 1990.
However, Karl Burke has a better record. He scored with Daring Destiny in 1994, and saddled a one-two through that mare and Always Alight in 1998. Keep a close eye on anything the ambitious Newmarket trainer sends here in the future.

NEWBURY, SATURDAY SEPTEMBER 16
MILL REEF STAKES (GROUP 2) TWO-YEAR-OLDS (6f)

YR	FORM	WINNER	WT	S.P.	DRAW	GOING	TRAINER	JOCKEY	FORM IN YEAR WN-RN	WN DIST.
90	12143	**TIME GENTLEMEN**	8.11	9-2	3	GD-FM	J.Dunlop	W.Carson	2-5	6f
91	101221	**SHOWBROOK**	9.01	4-1(SF)	3	GD-FM	R.Hannon	W.Carson	2-7	6f
92	12	**FOREST WIND**	8.11	11-2	4	GD	M.Moubarak	L.Dettori	1-2	6f
93	121	**POLISH LAUGHTER**	8.11	4-1(SF)	4	GD-SFT	B.Hanbury	W.Swinburn	2-3	6f
94	11144	**PRINCELY HUSH**	8.11	9-2	9	GD-SFT	M.Bell	M.Fenton	3-5	5f
95	21231	**KAHIR ALMAYDAN**	8.12	2-1F	3	GD-SFT	J.Dunlop	W.Carson	2-5	6f
96	21211	**INDIAN ROCKET**	8.12	100-30	1	GD-FM	J.Dunlop	R.Hills	3-5	6f
97	011	**ARKADIAN HERO**	8.12	4-9F	5	GD-SFT	L.Cumani	K.Fallon	2-3	6f
98	211031	**GOLDEN SILCA**	8.12	7-2	6	GD	M.Channon	S.Sanders	4-7	5,6f
99	24111	**PRIMO VALENTINO**	8.12	6-5F	2	GD-FM	P.Harris	M.Roberts	3-5	6f

FAVOURITES/SECOND FAVOURITES (strike rate and to a £1 stake): Favs. 25 per cent, -£5.36. **S.Favs. 17 per cent, -£2.**
TOP TRAINER (wins-runners, strike rate and to a £1 stake): **John Dunlop (3-3, 100 per cent,+£9.83).**

Introduction

Time Gentlemen, Showbrook, Forest Wind, Polish Laughter, Princely Hush, Kahir Almaydan, Indian Rocket and Arkadian Hero proved disappointing as three-year-olds. This is an awful long-term guide.

Ten year analysis

Weight/Rating: Showbrook and Golden Silca are the only horses to successfully carry a penalty over the past decade.

Form: This has always been a race for tough and experienced juveniles. Seven ran at least five times beforehand, eight winning a Group or Listed event over six furlongs.
Avoid any dropping back in trip – only two ran beyond six furlongs during their preparation.

Latest start: Eight ran in a Group or Listed race over six furlongs from August on their latest start, seven winning. This is obviously a vital factor.

Best trial: There are no outstanding trials, although it is worth noting that three consecutive winners - Kahir Almaydan, Indian Rocket and Arkadian Hero – landed the Ripon Champion Two-Year-Old Trophy (run on August 28).

Betting: The market has been a poor guide, both favourites and second favourites yielding a level-stakes loss.

Top trainer: John Dunlop has an unblemished three-from-three record in this race since 1990. Keep a close eye on anything he runs.

CURRAGH, SATURDAY SEPTEMBER 16
IRISH ST LEGER (GROUP 1) 1m 6f

YR	FORM	WINNER	AGE-WT	S.P.	GOING	TRAINER	JOCKEY	FORM IN YEAR WN-RN	WN DIST.
90	0-33412	**IBN BEY**	6 9.08	5-1(SF)	SFT	P.Cole	T.Quinn	1-5	12f
91	33-2101	**TURGEON**	5 9.08	3-1(SF)	GD-SFT	J.Pease(FR)	A.Cruz	2-4	15, 15.5f
92	211321	**MASHAALLAH**	4 9.08	11-4F	SFT	J.Gosden	S.Cauthen	4-7	10,12f
93	1-31012	**VINTAGE CROP**	6 9.08	9-2(SF)	GD-SFT	D.Weld(IR)	M.Kinane	2-5	14f
94	11-1221	**VINTAGE CROP**	7 9.08	7-4F	SFT	D.Weld(IR)	M.Kinane	2-4	14f
95	22-1330	**STRATEGIC CHOICE**	4 9.08	6-1	GD	P.Cole	T.Quinn	1-4	12f
96	43-2114	**OSCAR SCHINDLER**	4 9.08	4-1(SF)	GD-FM	K.Prendergast(IR)	S.Craine	2-4	12,13f
97	130-203	**OSCAR SCHINDLER**	5 9.08	2-1F	GD-SFT	K.Predergast(IR)	S.Craine	0-3	
98	1-13104	**KAYF TARA**	4 9.08	4-1(SF)	SFT	S. Bin Suroor	J.Reid	2-5	12,20f
99	41-1311	**KAYF TARA**	5 9.08	8-15F	SFT	S.Bin Suroor	L.Dettori	3-4	15,16f

AGE: (wins-runners): 3-Y-O: 0-24, 4-Y-O: 4-36:

FAVOURITES/SECOND FAVOURITES (strike rate and to a £1 stake): Favs. 40 per cent, +£1.03. **S.Favs. 31 per cent, +£9.50.**

Introduction

Opened to older horses in 1983, this numbers some cracking stayers among its winners, but is a Classic in name only.

Ten year analysis

Age: Three-year-olds have a miserable record, their last winner being Petite Ile back in 1989. By contrast, five and six-year-olds have excellent strike rates and are always worth a second glance.

Form: Seven – including the five English-trained winners – landed a Group race beforehand.

Latest start: Eight ran in a Group race from August on their latest start, three winning and four making the frame.

Best trial: Four ran in the Ascot Gold Cup, one winning, two making the frame and one finishing unplaced.

Betting: Favourites and second favourites have won nine of the last ten runnings. This is a race the market usually gets right.

Top trainer: Dermot Weld, Kevin Prendergast and Saeed Bin Suroor boast two winners apiece, courtesy of Vintage Crop, Oscar Schindler and Kayf Tara.
Paul Cole has also struck twice through the doughty duo Ibn Bey and Strategic Choice.

ASCOT, SATURDAY SEPTEMBER 23
TOTE HANDICAP (7f)

YR	FORM	WINNER	AGE-WT	RATING	S.P.	DRAW	GOING	TRAINER	JOCKEY	FORM IN YEAR WN-RN	WN DIST.
90	101012	**PONTENUOVO**	5 8.08	84	7-1(SF)	6	GD-FM	D.Elsworth	W.Carson	3-6	8,9f
91	30-4410	**NIGHT JAR**	4 8.09	85	33-1	9	GD-SFT	Ld Huntingdon	A.Munro	1-4	7f
92	420401	**SHARPALTO**	5 9.03	89	11-1(SF)	1	SFT	M.Reveley	M.Kinane	3-13	7f
93	300104	**YOUNG ERN**	3 8.12	96	25-1	17	GD-SFT	S.Dow	W.Ryan	1-11	7f
94	121113	**WIZARD KING**	3 8.07	92	13-2F	23	GD	Sir M.Precott	G.Duffield	4-7	7,8f
95	201302	**NIGHT DANCE**	3 7.10	84	20-1	6	GD-SFT	G.Lewis	A.Whelan	1-8	7f
96	202-301	**DECORATED HERO**	4 9.13	108	7-1(SF)	22	GD-FM	J.Gosden	L.Dettori	1-3	8f
97	011100	**JO MELL**	4 9.00	93	14-1	2	GD-FM	T.D.Easterby	O.Peslier	3-10	7,8f
98	-1124	**WHITE HEART**	3 8.09	95	10-1	11	GD	M.Johnston	D.Holland	2-4	6,7f
99	ABANDONED - WATERLOGGED										

AGE (wins-runners): 3-Y-O: 4-89, 4-Y-O: 3-68, **5-Y-O: 2-31,** 6-Y-O+: 0-36.
FAVOURITES/SECOND FAVOURITES (strike rate and to a £1 stake): Favs. 10 per cent, -£2.50. **S.Favs. 27 per cent, +£17.00.**
AVERAGE WINNING RATING: 92.

Introduction

Young Ern, Wizard King, Decorated Hero, Jo Mell and White Heart were more than capable of handling themselves in Listed/Group company. This is a red-hot handicap.

Ten year analysis

Age: No horse above the age of five has won to date. Avoid veterans when making your selection.

Weight/Rating Decorated Hero (rated 108, shouldering 9st 13lbs) is the odd man out. Him apart, none of the winners carried more than 9st 3lb, all eight being rated between 84 and 96.

Draw: Winners have come from both sides of the track.

Form: Nine won beforehand, eight landing a handicap from July. Proven form over this specialist trip is helpful – six won a seven-furlong handicap during their preparation.

Latest start: Seven ran in a handicap over seven furlongs or a mile from August on their latest start, two winning and three making the frame.

Betting: Only one favourite has been successful, and second favourites have a better record, producing a 17-point level-stakes profit since 1990.

Top trainer: There are no outstanding training trends on offer, although John Gosden's one winner and three placed horses will be of interest to each-way punters.

ASCOT, SATURDAY SEPTEMBER 23
FILLIES' MILE (GROUP 1) TWO-YEAR-OLD FILLIES (1m)

YR	FORM	WINNER	WT	S.P.	DRAW	GOING	TRAINER	JOCKEY	FORM IN YEAR WN-RN	WN DIST.
90	012	**SHAMSHIR**	8.10	11-2(SF)	12	GD-FM	L.Cumani	L.Dettori	1-3	7f
91	121	**CULTURE VULTURE**	8.10	5-2F	1	GD-SFT	P.Cole	T.Quinn	2-3	6f

92	103	**IVANKA**	8.10	6-1	1	SFT	C.Brittain	M.Roberts	1-3	6f
93	011	**FAIRY HEIGHTS**	8.10	11-1	2	GD-SFT	N.Callaghan	C.Asmussen	2-3	7f
94	1	**AQAARID**	8.10	11-2	5	GD-SFT	J.Dunlop	W.Carson	1-1	6f
95	1	**BOSRA SHAM**	8.10	10-11F	5	SFT	H.Cecil	Pat Eddery	1-1	6f
96	311	**REAMS OF VERSE**	8.10	5-1	2	GD	H.Cecil	M.Kinane	2-3	7,8f
97	13	**GLORIOSA**	8.10	10-1	4	GD-FM	L.Cumani	L.Dettori	1-2	7f
98	120	**SUNSPANGLED**	8.10	9-1	6	SFT	A.O'Brien(IR)	M.Kinane	1-3	7f
99	411	**TEGGIANO**	8.10	11-8F	1	HVY	C.Brittain	L.Dettori	2-3	6,8f

FAVOURITES/SECOND FAVOURITES (strike rate and to a £1 stake): **Favs. 30 per cent, -£2.22.** S.Favs. 8 per cent, -£5.50.

Introduction

While Bosra Sham and Reams Of Verse developed into outstanding performers, several other winners were bitterly disappointing as three-year-olds. This is an unreliable long-term guide.

Ten year analysis

Form: None had more than three outings beforehand, only two making their debut before July.
Nine won from July onward (five at Newmarket), six scoring over seven furlongs or a mile.

Latest start: Seven completed their preparation in a Group race from August, three winning and three making the frame.

Best trial: Five ran in the Group Three May Hill Stakes at Doncaster's St Leger Meeting, Teggiano and Reams Of Verse winning, while Shamshir, Ivanka and Gloriosa made the frame.

Betting: Both favourites and second favourites have produced a level-stakes loss. The market has been a poor guide.

Top trainers: Henry Cecil has the best record, sending out two winners and three placed horses since 1990. Luca Cumani and Clive Brittain (two winners each) are other trainers to keep an eye on.

ASCOT, SATURDAY SEPTEMBER 23
QUEEN ELIZABETH II STAKES (GROUP 1) (1m)

YR	FORM	WINNER	AGE-WT	RATING	S.P	DRAW	GOING	TRAINER	JOCKEY	FORM IN YEAR WN-RN	WN DIST.
90	23-1414	**MARKOFDISTINCTION**	4 9.04	-	6-1	1	GD-FM	L.Cumani	L.Dettori	2-4	8f
91	4-23341	**SELKIRK**	3 9.00	-	10-1	7	GD-SFT	I.Balding	R.Cochrane	1-5	8f

92	21-0212	**LAHIB**	4 9.04	-	8-1	9	SFT	J.Dunlop	W.Carson	1-4	8f
93	122213	**BIGSTONE**	3 9.00	-	100-30	6	GD-SFT	E.Lellouche(FR)	Pat Eddery	3-7	8f
94	022402	**MAROOF**	4 9.04	110	66-1	3	GD-SFT	R.Armstrong	R.Hills	0-6	
95	233122	**BAHRI**	3 8.11	125	5-2(SF)	1	GD-SFT	J.Dunlop	W.Carson	1-6	8f
96	21-101	**MARK OF ESTEEM**	3 8.11	129	10-3(SF)	5	GD-FM	S.Bin Suroor	L.Dettori	2-3	8f
97	3-41120	**AIR EXPRESS**	3 8.11	120	9-1	7	GD-FM	C.Brittain	O.Peslier	2-5	8f
98	4-13121	**DESERT PRINCE**	3 8.11	120	100-30F	1	GD	D.Loder	O.Peslier	3-5	7,8f
99	1-11011	**DUBAI MILLENNIUM**	3 8.11	122	4-9F	3	HVY	S.Bin Suroor	L.Dettori	4-5	8,10f

AGE (wins-runners): **3-Y-O: 7-47,** 4-Y-O: 3-26, 5-Y-O: 0-4, 6-Y-O+: 0-2.

FAVOURITES/SECOND FAVOURITES (strike rate and to a £1 stake): Favs. 20 per cent, -£3.67. **S.Favs. 17 per cent, -£4.17.**

AVERAGE WINNING RATING: 121.

Introduction

Won by outstanding horses like Markofdistinction, Selkirk, Mark Of Esteem, Desert Prince and Dubai Millennium, this race has flourished since being granted Group One status in 1987.

Ten year analysis

Age: This has been dominated by the younger generation, no horse above the age of four scoring since Hill Rise in 1966. With seven wins from 47 runners since 1990, three-year-olds have the best strike rate.

Weight/Rating: An average winning rating of 121 underlines the quality of horse required to win.

Form: Eight won a Group One or Two contest over a mile during their preparation.
It is also worth noting that six ran in a Group race over a mile at Royal Ascot, three winning and two finishing second.

Latest start: Seven ran in a mile Group race last time, three winning and three making the frame.

Best trial: Four ran in the St James's Palace Stakes at Royal Ascot, Bahri winning, Air Express and Desert Prince finishing second and Mark Of Esteem unplaced.

Betting: There have been a few surprise results – notably Maroof 66/1 in 1994 – and the market has been a poor guide.

Top trainers: Saeed Bin Suroor (two winners) and John Dunlop (two winners and one placed) have the best recent records.

ASCOT, SUNDAY SEPTEMBER 24
DIADEM STAKES (GROUP 2) (6f)

YR	FORM	WINNER	AGE-WT	RATING	S.P.	DRAW	GOING	TRAINER	JOCKEY	FORM IN YEAR WN-RN	WN DIST.
90	212210	**RON'S VICTORY**	3 8.11	-	13-2	11	GD-FM	A.Falourd	F.Head	2-6	5,6f
91	010040	**SHALFORD**	3 8.11	109	10-1	11	SFT	R.Hannon	A.Cruz	1-8	6f
92	1-34031	**WOLFHOUND**	3 8.11	114	4-1(SF)	10	SFT	J.Gosden	S.Cauthen	1-5	5f
93	1-10112	**CATRAIL**	3 8.11	124	10-11F	1	GD-SFT	J.Gosden	M.Roberts	3-5	6,7f
94	102141	**LAKE CONISTON**	3 8.11	119	85-40F	10	GD	G.Lewis	Pat Eddery	3-9	6f
95	331030	**COOL JAZZ**	4 9.00	102	33-1	1	GD-SFT	C.Brittain	C.Nakatani	1-9	6f
96	14-2100	**DIFFIDENT**	4 9.00	113	12-1	10	GD-FM	S.Bin Suroor	L.Dettori	1-4	7f
97	42-1211	**ELNADIM**	3 8.12	108	4-1(SF)	11	GD-FM	J.Dunlop	R.Hills	3-4	6f
98	2-14012	**BIANCONI**	3 8.12	108	7-1	5	GD	A.O'Brien(IR)	J.Murtagh	2-5	5.5,6f
99	101204	**BOLD EDGE**	4 9.04	116	12-1	7	HVY	R.Hannon	D.O'Neill	2-6	6f

AGE (wins-runners): **3-Y -O: 7-62,** 4-Y-O: 3-27, 5-Y-O: 0-14, 6-Y-O+: 0-19.
FAVOURITES/SECOND FAVOURITES (strike rate and to a £1 stake): Favs. 20 per cent, -£4.96. **S.Favs. 17 per cent, -£2.**
AVERAGE WINNING RATING: 113.

Introduction

This is run a shade close to the Prix de l'Abbaye to attract the very best sprinters. That said, it has been won by some top-class horses, notably Lake Coniston and Elnadim.

Ten year analysis

Age: No horse aged five or above has scored since Creetown in 1978. Restrict your selection to three and four-year-olds.

Weight/Rating: Bold Edge is the only recent winner to have carried a penalty. This is a race for unpenalised runners.

Form: Eight scored over six furlongs during their preparation. However, it is worth noting that two won and five were placed over seven furlongs or beyond. Do not be afraid to support a horse that stays beyond this trip.
Proven Group form is a big plus – three won and four finished placed in that sphere earlier in their year.

Latest start: Six ran in a six-furlong Group race last time, only one winning while three made the frame.

Best trial: Five ran in Haydock's Group One Stanley Leisure Sprint Cup, three making the frame and two finishing unplaced. Keep a close eye on any that shaped well in that contest.

Betting: Favourites and second favourites show a level-stakes loss – the market is a poor guide.

Top trainer: John Gosden (two winners and three placed) has produced consistent results. Anything he runs should perform creditably.

ASCOT, SUNDAY SEPTEMBER 24
RITZ CLUB HANDICAP (1m 4f)

YR	FORM	WINNER	AGE-WT	RATING	S.P.	DRAW	GOING	TRAINER	JOCKEY	FORM IN YEAR WN-RN	WN DIST.
90	203144	**SECRET SOCIETY**	3 8.00	82	20-1	12	GD-FM	M.Camacho	N.Connorton	2-9	8,12f
91	000113	**TIDEMARK**	4 8.10	91	10-1	7	SFT	L.Cumani	L.Dettori	2-7	12f
92	202101	**QUICK RANSOM**	4 9.01	84	14-1	8	SFT	M.Johnston	D.McKeown	3-9	12,14f
93	230210	**LEAGUE LEADER**	3 8.10	88	10-1	1	GD-SFT	M.Stoute	W.Carson	2-8	12f
94	1022-43	**WHITECHAPEL**	6 8.05	84	6-1	8	GD-SFT	Ld Huntingdon	M.Hills	0-2	
95	4-20022	**TAUFAN'S MELODY**	4 9.01	100	20-1	2	SFT	Lady Herries	R.Cochrane	0-5	
96	2-00130	**BETTER OFFER**	4 9.06	98	9-1	14	GD	G.Harwood	M.Kinane	1-5	12f
*97	-3110	**RIDAIYMA**	3 8.04	92	9-2F	12	GD-FM	L.Cumani	K.Darley	2-4	12f
98	240401	**RAISE A PRINCE**	5 8.08	94	8-1	5	SFT	S.Woods	N.Callan	2-7	12,13f
99	210-121	**VICIOUS CIRCLE**	5 9.09	101	13-2	1	HVY	L.Cumani	L.Dettori	2-3	10,14f

*TAUFAN'S MELODY, 6 9.10, 20-1, Lady Herries, J.Reid, finished first, disqualified and placed second.

AGE (wins-runners): 3-Y-O: 3-53, 4-Y-O: 4-59, **5-Y-O: 2-27**, 6-Y-O+: 1-22.
FAVOURITES/SECOND FAVOURITES (strike rate and to a £1 stake): **Favs. 7 per cent, -£7.50.** S.Favs. 0 per cent, -£14.
AVERAGE WINNING RATING: 91.
TOP TRAINER (wins-runners, strike rate and to a £1 stake): **Luca Cumani (3-13, 23 per cent, +£13).**

Introduction

Once again, it often takes a Listed or Group-class runner to land this valuable handicap. Tidemark, Quick Ransom, Taufan's Melody, Ridaiyma and Vicious Circle all fall into that category.

Ten year analysis

Age: Winners are spread across the age groups, five-year-olds boasting the best strike rate.

Weight/Rating: The standard of this race has improved year-on-year, none of the last five being rated below 92. It could pay to side with those rated slightly above our ten-year average (91).

Draw: Those drawn low may have a fractional advantage on soft ground, as the runners usually race under the trees on the outside of the track in the back straight.

Form: Seven won at least twice during their preparation, six scoring over 12-14 furlongs from August.
Perhaps more importantly, seven ran at York's Ebor Meeting, where two won, four finished placed and one unplaced. Form at that fixture is a huge bonus.

Latest start: Eight ran in a 12-14 furlong handicap from August on their latest start, five at the Ebor Meeting.

Best trial: Unsurprisingly, the Ebor Handicap is our best trial. Quick Ransom and Vicious Circle won that prestigious contest, while Tidemark finished second and Better Offer seventh.

Betting: Only one first or second favourite has obliged. The market has been a disastrous guide.

Top trainer: Luca Cumani, who has a wonderful record in valuable middle-distance handicaps, rules the roost. The Newmarket man has sent out three winners and two placed horses from 13 runners since 1990.

ASCOT, SUNDAY SEPTEMBER 24
ROYAL LODGE STAKES (GROUP 2) TWO-YEAR-OLD COLTS AND GELDINGS (1m)

YR	FORM	WINNER	WT	S.P.	DRAW	GOING	TRAINER	JOCKEY	FORM IN YEAR WN-RN	WN DIST.
90	231	**MUJAAZIF**	8.10	11-2(SF)	8	GD-FM	M.Stoute	W.Swinburn	1-3	8f
91	1222	**MADE OF GOLD**	8.10	4-1(SF)	4	GD-SFT	M.Moubarak	A.Cruz	1-4	6f
92	02	**DESERT SECRET**	8.11	12-1	7	SFT	M.Stoute	Pat Eddery	0-2	
93	1310	**MISTER BAILEYS**	8.10	10-3JF	7	GD-SFT	M.Johnston	L.Dettori	2-4	6,7f
94	211	**ELTISH**	8.10	7-4F	2	GD-SFT	H.Cecil	Pat Eddery	2-3	7f
95	121	**MONS**	8.11	7-2	6	GD-SFT	L.Cumani	L.Dettori	2-3	6,7f
96	211	**BENNY THE DIP**	8.11	9-4F	3	GD	J.Gosden	W.Swinburn	2-3	7f
97	141	**TEAPOT ROW**	8.11	9-1	4	GD-FM	J.Toller	S.Sanders	2-3	6,7f
98	14011	**MUTAAHAB**	8.11	5-1	6	SFT	E.Dunlop	R.Hills	3-5	6,7,8f
99	11	**ROYAL KINGDOM**	8.11	10-11F	5	HVY	A.O'Brien(IR)	M.Kinane	2-2	7f

FAVOURITES/SECOND FAVOURITES (strike rate and to a £1 stake): **Favs. 36 per cent, +£1.24,** S.Favs. 17 per cent, -£1.50.

Introduction

This race has a mixed reputation as a long-term guide. While several recent winners were very disappointing as three-year-olds, Mister Baileys and Benny The Dip both went on to land a Classic.

Ten year analysis

Form: Mutaahab is the odd man out in the list of recent winners. Him apart, none of the successful horses made their debut before May, each having a two-four start preparation.
The last seven scored over seven furlongs, while five had already landed a Group or Listed event.

Latest start: Seven – including the last six – were successful on their latest start.

Best trial: There are no outstanding trials, although three ran in the Group Three Champagne Lanson Vintage Stakes at Glorious Goodwood. Mister Baileys and Eltish won that event, while Made Of Gold finished second.

Betting: Favourites have a fair record, but the market has not been a great guide.

Top trainer: Once again, there are no outstanding trainer trends, Sir Michael Stoute's two winners and one placed being the best result.

ASCOT, SUNDAY SEPTEMBER 24
MAIL ON SUNDAY MILE FINAL HANDICAP (1m)

YR	FORM	WINNER	AGE-WT	RATING	S.P.	DRAW	GOING	TRAINER	JOCKEY	FORM IN YEAR WN-RN	WN DIST.
90	220031	**ROSEATE LODGE**	4 8.06	-	5-1JF	9	GD-FM	R.Armstrong	L.Dettori	1-9	8f
91	13-0000	**SELAAH**	4 9.02	90	11-1	3	GD-FM	M.Stoute	Pat Eddery	0-4	
92	00/2011	**RAMBO'S HALL**	7 8.12	88	9-2JF	7	SFT	J.Glover	D.McKeown	2-4	10f
93	000120	**RAMBO'S HALL**	8 9.07	99	11-2(SF)	6	GD-SFT	J.Glover	P.Robinson	1-7	10f
94	NO RACE										
95	034210	**MO-ADDAB**	5 8.13	73	25-1	9	SFT	A.Stewart	M.Roberts	1-7	8f
96	200010	**AMRAK AJEEB**	4 10.00	99	33-1	2	GD	B.Hanbury	M.Rimmer	2-10	8,10f
97	040120	**GULF SHAADI**	5 8.06	74	20-1	10	GD-FM	E.Alston	S.Sanders	4-21	7,8f
98	102010	**SILKEN DALLIANCE**	3 7.07	74	10-1(SF)	21	SFT	Ld Huntingdon	A.Nicholls	2-7	6,8f
99	002004	**INDIUM**	5 8.05	74	14-1	19	HVY	W.Musson	Pat Eddery	0-10	

AGE (wins-runners): 3-Y-O: 1-39, 4-Y-O: 3-46, **5-Y-O: 3-37,** 6-Y-O+: 2-35.
FAVOURITES/SECOND FAVOURITES (Strike rate and to a £1 stake): Favs. 14 per cent, -£2.50. **S.Favs. 13 per cent, +£2.50**
AVERAGE WINNING RATING: 84.

Introduction

This fiercely-competitive handicap usually falls to a tough and experienced performer. The list of recent winners lacks class, but not heart.

Ten year analysis

Age: Winners have come from every age group, although it is worth noting that only one three-year-old has been successful.

Weight/Rating: Only one of the nine winners since 1990 carried less than 8st 5lbs. This is not a race for feather weights.

Draw: Winners have come from both sides of the track.

Form: Seven won beforehand, six scoring from August. Seven had at least seven outings beforehand, indicating that your selection must be battle-hardened.

Latest start: Six ran in a seven-furlong or mile handicap from September last time, only one winning.

Betting: With winners being returned at 20/1, 25/1 and 33/1, this is a race for value seekers.

NEWMARKET, TUESDAY SEPTEMBER 26
CHEVELEY PARK STAKES (GROUP 1) TWO-YEAR-OLD FILLIES (6f)

YR	FORM	WINNER	WT	S.P.	DRAW	GOING	TRAINER	JOCKEY	FORM IN YEAR WN-RN	WN DIST.
90	1011	**CAPRICCIOSA**	8.11	7-1	4	GD	M.V.O'Brien(IR)	J.Reid	3-4	5,6f
91	111	**MARLING**	8.11	15-8F	4	GD-FM	G.Wragg	W.Swinburn	3-3	5f
92	211	**SAYYEDATI**	8.11	5-2(SF)	3	GD	C.Brittain	W.Swinburn	2-3	6,7f
93	1001	**PROPHECY**	8.11	12-1	1	GD-SFT	J.Gosden	Pat Eddery	2-4	5,6f
94	0123	**GAY GALLANTA**	8.11	14-1	2	GD	M.Stoute	Pat Eddery	1-4	5f
95	111	**BLUE DUSTER**	8.11	4-5F	5	GD	D.Loder	M.Kinane	3-3	5,6f
96	131	**PAS DE REPONSE**	8.11	7-1	3	GD	C.Head(FR)	F.Head	2-3	5.5,6f
97	112	**EMBASSY**	8.11	5-2(SF)	3	GD-FM	D.Loder	K.Fallon	2-3	6f
98	211424	**WANNABE GRAND**	8.11	3-1F	7	GD	J.Noseda	Pat Eddery	2-7	6f
99	012	**SEAZUN**	8.11	10-1	8	GD-SFT	M.Channon	T.Quinn	1-3	5f

FAVOURITES/SECOND FAVOURITES (Strike rate and to a £1 stake): **Favs. 30 per cent, -£1.33. S.Favs. 20 per cent, -£3**

Introduction

While Marling and Sayyedati established themselves as top-class performers, many recent winners of this race proved extremely disappointing as three-year-olds. For example, Prophecy, Blue Duster and Embassy clearly failed to fulfil their early potential. Success here is no passport to greater glory.

Ten year analysis

Form: None had less than three previous starts, eight winning at least twice. However, it is more important to note that eight had already landed a Group race.
Only two ran beyond six furlongs, both taking part in the seven-furlong Moyglare Stud Stakes at The Curragh.

Latest start: Eight ran in a Group race on their latest start, five winning and three making the frame.

Best trials: There are several useful trials: Three ran in Royal Ascot's Queen Mary Stakes, each winning. Four took part in the Princess Margaret Stakes (run at Ascot on July 29), two winning, one making the frame and one finishing unplaced. Finally, four took part in York's Lowther Stakes, three making the frame and one finishing out of the money. All these races are Group events, underlining the value of form in that sphere.

Betting: Favourites and second favourites have a disappointing record. With winners returning at 10/1, 12/1 and 14/1, shock results are commonplace.

Top trainer: David Loder – who has only held a licence since 1992 - has already sent out two winners and two placed horses. Now based at Evry in France, anything he sends in pursuit of this prestigious prize must be treated with respect.

NEWMARKET, THURSDAY SEPTEMBER 29
MIDDLE PARK STAKES (GROUP 1) TWO-YEAR-OLD COLTS (6f)

YR	FORM	WINNER	WT	S.P.	DRAW	GOING	TRAINER	JOCKEY	FORM IN YEAR WN-RN	WN DIST.
90	412	**LYCIUS**	9.00	13-8F	4	GD	A.Fabre(FR)	C.Asmussen	1-3	7f
91	1111	**RODRIGO DE TRIANO**	9.00	EV F	1	GD-FM	P.Chapple-Hyam	W.Carson	4-4	6,7f
92	111	**ZIETEN**	9.00	5-2(SF)	3	GD	A.Fabre(FR)	S.Cauthen	3-3	5,5.5,6f

93	11113	**FIRST TRUMP**	9.00	6-1	5	GD	G.Wragg	M.Hills	4-5	6f
94	311142	**FARD**	9.00	33-1	2	GD-FM	D.Morley	W.Carson	3-6	5,6f
95	111	**ROYAL APPLAUSE**	8.11	3-1(SF)	5	GD	B.Hills	W.Swinburn	3-3	5,6f
96	211	**BAHAMIAN BOUNTY**	8.11	7-4F	2	GD-FM	D.Loder	L.Dettori	2-3	5,6f
97	20123	**HAYIL**	8.11	14-1	4	GD-FM	D.Morley	R.Hills	1-5	6f
98	11	**LUJAIN**	8.11	8-11F	2	GD	D.Loder	L.Dettori	2-2	6f
99	241111	**PRIMO VALENTINO**	8.11	10-3(SF)	1	GD-SFT	P.Harris	Pat Eddery	4-6	6f

FAVOURITES/SECOND FAVOURITES (Strike rate and to a £1 stake): **Favs. 40 per cent, -£0.90.** S.Favs. 27 per cent, +£0.83.

Introduction

This is another unreliable long-term guide. While Rodrigo de Triano developed into a star, First Trump, Fard, Bahamian Bounty, Hayil and Lujain were very disappointing as three-year-olds.

Ten year analysis

Form: Avoid greenhorns - only one of the last ten had less than three previous outings. All ten had won (nine over six furlongs) six scoring at least three times.

Latest start: Seven ran in a Group race from August on their latest start, five winning and two making the frame.

Betting: Upsets can occur – witness Fard (33/1) and Hayil (14/1) – but the market is usually a fair guide. Favourites and second favourites have won seven of the last ten runnings.

Top trainers: Andre Fabre (two winners and one placed) and David Loder (two winners) have the best records. With that in mind, it would be no surprise to see this prize snaffled by a series of cross-Channel raiders in the years ahead.

NEWMARKET, SATURDAY SEPTMBER 30
SUN CHARIOT STAKES (GROUP 2) FILLIES AND MARES (1m 2f)

YR	FORM	WINNER	AGE-WT	RATING	S.P.	DRAW	GOING	TRAINER	JOCKEY	FORM IN YEAR WN-RN	WN DIST.
90	-11012	**KARTAJANA**	3 8.11	-	11-10F	7	GD-FM	M.Stoute	W.Swinburn	3-5	10f
91	-142	**RISTNA**	3 8.08	-	4-1	3	GD-FM	J.Gosden	W.Carson	1-3	8f
92	210-041	**RED SLIPPERS**	3 8.08	-	6-4F	2	GD-SFT	L.Cumani	L.Dettori	1-3	10f

93	124323	**TALENTED**	3 8.08	102	4-1	8	GD-SFT	J.Dunlop	W.Carson	1-6	10f
94	-101	**LA CONFEDERATION**	3 8.08	-	5-1(SF)	1	GD	D.Loder	K.Darley	2-3	8,10f
95	402243	**WARNING SHADOWS**	3 8.08	111	6-1	5	GD-FM	C.Brittain	K.Darley	1-9	7f
96	11-21	**LAST SECOND**	3 8.11	114	9-4F	8	GD-FM	Sir M.Prescott	G.Duffield	1-2	10f
97	1-1	**ONE SO WONDERFUL**	8.08	-	5-2(SF)	6	GD-FM	L.Cumani	J.Reid	1-1	8f
98	-141	**KISSOGRAM**	3 8.08	106	5-4F	3	GD	L.Cumani	J.Reid	2-3	8f
99	21-1220	**LADY IN WAITING**	4 8.13	108	5-1(SF)	4	SFT	P.Cole	J.Fortune	1-4	10f

AGE (wins-runners): **3-Y-O: 9-51,** 4-Y-O: 1-15, 5-Y-O: 0-1, 6-Y-O+: 0-2.
FAVOURITES/SECOND FAVOURITES (strike rate and to a £1 stake): Favs. 40 per cent, -£0.10. **S.Favs. 27 per cent, +£4.50.**
TOP TRAINER (winners-runners, strike rate and to a £1 stake): **Luca Cumani (3-5, 60 per cent, +£3.25).**
AVERAGE WINNING RATING: 108.

Introduction

As an average win rating of 108 suggests, this is not the most competitive Group Two in the programme book.

Ten year analysis

Age: Three-year-olds have won nine of the last ten runnings and are strongly favoured.

Form/Rating: None of the recent winners were rated above 114.

Form: All ten won beforehand. Four won and five finishing placed in a Group or Listed race around ten furlongs from July - smart form around this trip seems essential.

Latest start: Five won last time, only one finishing unplaced. Avoid those who may be on a downward spiral after a long season.

Best trial: Five ran in Goodwood's Nassau Stakes (run on August 5), Kartajana and Last Second winning, while Warning Shadows, Kissogram and Lady In Waiting were placed.

Betting: Favourites and second favourites have won seven of the last ten renewals, both showing a level-stakes profit.

Top trainer: Luca Cumani has an excellent record. His five runners since 1990 have yielded three winners, two placed horses and a level-stakes profit.

NEWMARKET, SATURDAY SEPTEMBER 30
CAMBRIDGESHIRE HANDICAP (1m 1f)

YR	FORM	WINNER	AGE-WT	RATING	S.P.	DRAW	GOING	TRAINER	JOCKEY	FORM IN YEAR WN-RN	WN DIST.
90	0-1201	**RISEN MOON**	3 8.09	90	7-1F	2	GD-FM	B.Hills	S.Cauthen	2-4	7f
91	124042	**MELLOTTIE**	6 9.01	92	10-1(SF)	27	GD-FM	M.Reveley	J.Lowe	2-7	8,10f
92	3/20111	**RAMBO'S HALL**	7 9.03	92	9-2F	7	GD-SFT	J.Glover	D.McKeown	3-5	8,10f
93	313212	**PENNY DROPS**	4 7.13	84	7-1F	18	GD-SFT	Ld Huntingdon	D.Harrison	2-6	8f
94	-04011	**HALLING**	3 8.08	93	8-1JF	24	GD	J.Gosden	L.Dettori	2-5	10f
95	-01111	**CAP JULUCA**	3 9.10	107	11-1(SF)	26	GD-FM	R.Charlton	R.Hughes	4-5	8,10f
96	240331	**CLIFTON FOX**	4 8.02	85	14-1	17	GD-FM	J.Glover	N.Day	2-9	9,10f
97	20311-1	**PASTERNAK**	4 9.01	91	4-1F	17	GD-FM	Sir M.Prescott	G.Duffield	1-1	10f
98	003133	**LEAR SPEAR**	3 7.13	90	20-1	33	GD	D.Elsworth	N.Pollard	1-8	8f
*99	1-13001	**SHE'S OUR MARE**	6 7.12	78	11-1	14	SFT	A.J.Martin(IR)	F.Norton	2-5	8f

*RUN ON THE JULY COURSE. OVER 1m 2f

AGE (wins-runners): 3-Y-O: 4-111, 4-Y-O: 3-106, 5-Y-O: 0-71, **6-Y-O+: 3-55.**

FAVOURITES/SECOND FAVOURITES (Strike rate and to a £1 stake): **Favs. 38 per cent, +£22.50.** S.Favs. 13 per cent, +£8.00.

AVERAGE WINNING RATING: 90.

Introduction

It usually pays to follow the winner of the Cambridgeshire. Halling went on to land numerous Group Ones, while Mellottie, Penny Drops and Lear Spear also established themselves as high-class performers.

Ten year analysis

Age: Age is not overly important, although it is worth noting that five-year-olds have drawn a blank.

Weight/Rating: Only one recent winner carried above 9st 3lbs, or was rated above 93.

Draw: On the whole high numbers seem marginally favoured. Excluding last year's race (run on the July Course), seven came from stalls numbered 17-33.

Form: All ten won beforehand, eight scoring at least twice between seven and ten furlongs. Note that eight won from August onward.

Latest start: Eight had their latest start from September, five winning and two making the frame in a handicap.

Betting: Surprisingly, this has been a fair race for followers of the market. Favourites and second favourites show a healthy level-stakes profit since 1990.

Top trainer: Jeremy Glover has an outstanding record, saddling two winners and a placed horse from just four runners since 1990. Also responsible for the 1989 winner Rambo's Hall, he is definitely the trainer to watch.

REDCAR, SATURDAY SEPTEMBER 30
REDCAR TWO-YEAR-OLD TROPHY (6f)

YR	FORM	WINNER	WT	S.P.	DRAW	GOING	TRAINER	JOCKEY	FORM IN YEAR WN-RN	WN DIST
90	30011	**CHIPAYA**	8-05	7-1(SF)	1	GD	J.Fanshawe	W.Carson	2-5	6f
91	42311	**CASTEDDU**	8-01	4-1(SF)	2	GD-FM	J.Payne	A.Munro	2-5	7f
92	330142	**PIPS PRIDE**	8-05	6-1(SF)	5	HVY	R.Hannon	D.MCcKeown	3-8	5,6f
93	120	**CAPE MERINO**	7-07	33-1	4	SFT	A.Smith	J.Lowe	1-3	5f
94	012002	**MAID FOR WALKING**	7-13	7-1(SF)	13	GD	D.Loder	D.Harrison	2-8	5,6f
95	11	**BLUE IRIS**	8-02	6-1	14	FM	M.Jarvis	P.Robinson	2-2	5f
96	111402	**PROUD NATIVE**	8.07	13-2	5	GD-FM	A.Jarvis	W.Ryan	3-6	5,6f
97	2	**GRAZIA**	8.02	7-2F	3	GD-FM	Sir M.Prescott	G.Duffield	0-1	
98	11224	**PIPALONG**	7.13	5-2F	8	SFT	T.D.Easterby	L.Charnock	2-5	5f
99	211421	**KHASAYL**	8.08	9-4F	2	GD	P.Walwyn	T.Sprake	3-6	5,6f

FAVOURITES/SECOND FAVOURITES (strike rate and to a £1 stake): Favs. 30 per cent, +£1.25. **S.Favs. 44 per cent, +£19.**

Introduction

Inaugurated in 1989, this race is a sound long-term guide. Pips Pride, Proud Native, Grazia and Pipalong developed into smart sprinters after winning, and their successor could be more than a nippy juvenile.

Ten year analysis

Weight/Rating: None of the winners carried above 8st 8lbs. With each runner's weight being determined by the median price of its sire's progeny rather than racing ability, those at the head of the list often face a stiff task.

Draw: Eight of the winners were drawn in stalls 1-8. Low numbers seem to hold the advantage.

Form: Seven had at least five outings beforehand, indicating that experienced juveniles have an edge.
Eight scored at least twice during their preparation, while three won and three made the frame in a Group or Listed event.
It must also be pointed out that fillies have won seven of the last ten renewals. This is a good advert for Girl Power.

Latest start: Nine had their latest start from September, three winning and five finishing placed.

Betting: The market has been an excellent guide. Favourites have won the last three renewals, while second favourites boast a 19-point level-stakes profit.

Top trainer: Richard Hannon landed the inaugural running with Osario in 1989, and has gone on to saddle another winner (Pips Pride) and seven placed horses.

LONGCHAMP, SUNDAY OCTOBER 1
PRIX DE L'ABBAYE DE LONGCHAMP (GROUP 1) (5f)

YR	FORM	WINNER	AGE-WT	S.P.	GOING	TRAINER	JOCKEY	FORM IN YEAR WN-RN	WN DIST.
90	121111	**DAYJUR**	3 9.11	1-10F	GD	W.Hern	W.Carson	5-7	5,6f
91	0/110-1	**KEEN HUNTER**	4 9.11	12-1	GD-SFT	J.Gosden	S.Cauthen	1-1	6f
92	221122	**MR BROOKS**	5 9.11	9-10F	SFT	R.Hannon	L.Piggott	3-7	5,6,6.5f
93	431113	**LOCHSONG**	5 9.08	2-1(SF)	HVY	I.Balding	L.Dettori	3-8	5f
94	111010	**LOCHSONG**	6 9.07	7-10F	GD-SFT	I.Balding	L.Dettori	4-6	5f
95	113111	**HEVER GOLF ROSE**	4 9.07	3.1-1	SFT	T.J.Naughton	J.Weaver	7-11	5,6f
96	121211	**KISTENA**	3 9.08	14.6-1	GD-SFT	C.Head(FR)	O.Doleuze	4-7	5,5.5,6f
97	13140-3	**CARMINE LAKE**	3 9.08	16.8-1	GD-FM	P.Chapple-Hyam	J.Reid	0-1	
98	004020	**MY BEST VALENTINE**	8 9.10	33-1	SFT	V.Soane	R.Cochrane	0-9	
99	220011	**AGNES WORLD**	4 9.10	7-1	HVY	H.Mori(JPN)	Y.Take	2-7	6f

AGE: (wins-runners): 2-Y-O: 0-8, 3-Y-O: 3-41, 4-Y-O: 3-35, 5-Y-O: 2-15, **6-Y-O+: 2-11**
FAVOURITES/SECOND FAVOURITES (to a £1 stake): **Favs. -£6.30.** S.Favs. -£7.

Introduction

The French find it virtually impossible to keep this prize at home. Over the past decade only Kistena has won for the home team, while English raiders have scored on eight occasions.

Ten year analysis

Age: There is no age bias, although two-year-olds understandably find this a tough nut to crack.

Form: Seven won a Group race earlier in their year, but it is more interesting to note that six landed at least three Group/Listed sprints during their preparation.

Latest start: Avoid any who disappointed last time – five won and three made the frame on their latest start.

Best trial: York's Group One Nunthorpe Stakes is our best trial. Six ran in that race, two winning, two making the frame and two finishing unplaced.

Betting: There have been plenty of surprise results, Keen Hunter (12/1), Kistena (14.6/1), Carmine Lake (16.8/1) and My Best Valentine (33/1) all catching punters unaware. Do not be afraid to look beyond the obvious.

Top trainer: Ian Balding has sent out two winners from just three runners since 1990, but the safest method of selection is to stick with English-trained runners. They have won eight of the last ten renewals.

LONGCHAMP, SUNDAY OCTOBER 1
PRIX DE L'ARC DE TRIOMPHE (GROUP 1) (1m 4f)

									FORM IN YEAR	
YR	FORM	WINNER	AGE-WT	S.P.	DRAW	GOING	TRAINER	JOCKEY	WN-RN	WN DIST.
90	112101	SAUMAREZ	3 8.11	15-1	10	GD	N.Clement(FR)	G.Mosse	4-6	8,10f
91	112121	SUAVE DANCER	3 8.11	3.7-1(SF)	12	GD-SFT	J.Hammond(FR)	C.Asmussen	4-6	10,12f
92	01-1432	SUBOTICA	4 9.04	8.8-1	14	SFT	A.Fabre(FR)	T.Jarnet	1-4	10f
93	100211	URBAN SEA	4 9.01	37-1	9	HVY	J.Lesbordes(FR)	E.Saint-Martin	3-6	10f
94	120111	CARNEGIE	3 8.11	3-1JF	2	GD-SFT	A.Fabre(FR)	T.Jarnet	4-6	10,12f
95	1-11	LAMMTARRA	3 8.11	2.1-1F	7	SFT	S.Bin Suroor	L.Dettori	2-2	12f
96	111011	HELISSIO	3 8.11	1.8-1F	5	GD-SFT	E.Lellouche(FR)	O.Peslier	5-6	10,10.5,11,12f
97	13-1112	PEINTRE CELEBRE	3 8.11	2.2-1F	2	GD-FM	A.Fabre(FR)	O.Peslier	3-4	10,12f
98	-111	SAGAMIX	3 8.11	5-2F	7	SFT	A.Fabre(FR)	O.Peslier	3-3	12f
99	1-12111	MONTJEU	3 8.11	6-4F	4	HVY	J.Hammond(FR)	M.Kinane	4-5	10,12f

AGE: (wins-runners): **3-Y-O: 8-83,** 4-Y-O: 2-59, 5-Y-O: 0-25, 6-Y-O+: 0-.
FAVOURITES/SECOND FAVOURITES (to a £1 stake): **Favs. +£8.10.** S.Favs. -£5.30.

Introduction

One of the highlights of the season, this race has witnessed some tremendous performances, including Montjeu's flying finish to thwart El Condor Pasa 12 months ago. His victory made it nine wins for France in the past decade, underlining that the home team are always hard to beat in the Arc.

Ten year analysis

Age: Three-year-olds have a wonderful record, winning eight times since 1990 and landing the last six renewals. It is also worth noting that no horse above the age of four has scored since Tony Bin in 1988.

Draw: Much is made of the significance of the draw and low numbers may have a slight edge. However, a high number does not spell disaster.

Form: Eight had a four-six start preparation. Nine won at least twice, the same number landing a Group One or Two event, seven around ten furlongs.

Latest start: Eight completed their preparation in a middle-distance Group race during September, six winning and two finishing second.

Best trials: The Prix Niel (run at Longchamp on September 10) is our best trial. Five ran in that contest, four winning and one finishing second. Other key trials are the French Derby - three won and one finished unplaced – and Prix Greffulhe – three won and one unplaced.

Betting: Favourites have enjoyed a tremendous run, winning the last six renewals. The market has been an excellent guide recently.

Top trainer: French-trained horses have ruled the roost since 1990, Lammtarra being the only successful raider. Andre Fabre is the pick of the French handlers during this period, saddling four winners. His runners are obviously worth a second glance.

NEWMARKET, SATURDAY OCTOBER 14
CHALLENGE STAKES (GROUP 2) (7f)

YR	FORM	WINNER	AGE-WT	RATING	S.P.	DRAW	GOING	TRAINER	JOCKEY	FORM IN YEAR WN-RN	WN DIST
90	400132	**SALLY ROUS**	3 8.08	-	11-4(SF)	8	GD	G.Wragg	G.Carter	1-6	7f
91	3-11004	**MYSTIKO**	3 9.00	-	9-4F	1	GD-FM	C.Brittain	M.Roberts	2-5	7,8f
92	1-10213	**SELKIRK**	4 9.03	-	5-6F	4	GD-FM	I.Balding	R.Cochrane	2-5	8f
93	101121	**CATRAIL**	3 8.11	124	4-5F	4	GD-SFT	J.Gosden	M.Roberts	4-6	6,7f
94	443-200	**ZIETEN**	4 9.00	-	13-2	3	GD	J.Gosden	L.Dettori	0-3	
95	033114	**HARAYIR**	3 8.12	118	13-8F	8	GD-FM	W.Hern	W.Carson	3-8	7,8f
96	1-21244	**CHARNWOOD FOREST**	4 9.04	122	15-8F	8	GD-FM	S.Bin Suroor	L.Dettori	1-5	8f
97	10-2441	**KAHAL**	3 8.12	109	9-2(SF)	4	GD	S.Bin Suroor	L.Dettori	1-4	7f
98	0-10413	**DECORATED HERO**	6 9.04	118	11-2(SF)	4	GD	J.Gosden	O.Peslier	2-5	7f
99	10431	**SUSU**	6 8.11	-	8-1	10	GD	Sir M.Stoute	K.Fallon	2-5	7f

AGE (wins-runners): 3-Y-O: 5-49, 4-Y-O: 3-21, 5-Y-O: 0-10, **6-Y-O+: 2-6.**
FAVOURITES/SECOND FAVOURITES (strike rate and to a £1 stake): **Favs. 50 per cent, +£2.37.** S.Favs. 21 per cent, -£1.75.
AVEAGE WINNIGN RATING: 118.
TOP TRAINERS (wins-runners, strike rate and to a £1 stake): **John Gosden (3-6, 50 per cent, +£9.80).**

Introduction

The profile of this race has improved in recent seasons, crack horses like Mystiko, Selkirk, Harayir and Charnwood Forest helping to enhance its image.

Ten year analysis

Age: Age is no bar to success, those aged six and above having the best strike rate.

Weight/Rating: As Mystiko, Selkirk, Harayir and Charnwood Forest have proved, penalties can be carried successfully.

Form: Seven won a Group race between six furlongs and a mile during their preparation.

Latest start: Seven ran in a Group race from September last time, only one winning while six made the frame.

Betting: Favourites boast an excellent 50 per cent strike rate.

Top trainer: Saeed Bin Suroor has sent out two winners and three placed horses over the past four seasons. However, John Gosden has the best training record, sending out three winners and two placed horses from just six runners since 1990.

NEWMARKET, SATURDAY OCTOBER 14
CESAREWITCH HANDICAP (2m 2f)

YR	FORM	WINNER	AGE-WT	RATING	S.P.	DRAW	GOING	TRAINER	JOCKEY	FORM IN YEAR WN-RN	WN DIST
90	13-2101	TRAINGLOT	3 7.12	81	13-2(SF)	16	GD	J.FitzGerald	W.Carson	2-4	14,16f
91	002104	GO SOUTH	7 7.11	63	33-1	14	GD-FM	J.Jenkins	N.Carlisle	1-10	18f
92	1-1310	VINTAGE CROP	5 9.06	102	5-1F	10	GD-FM	D.Weld(IR)	W.Swinburm	2-4	14f
93	204-213	AAHSAYLAD	7 8.12	81	12-1(SF)	21	GD	J.White	J.Williams	1-3	18f
94	0-20101	CAPTAIN'S GUEST	4 9.09	92	25-1	28	GD-FM	G.Harwood	A.Clark	2-5	16f
95	12303-4	OLD RED	5 7.11	66	11-1	18	GD-FM	M.Reveley	L.Charnock	0-1	
96	040-021	INCHCAILLOCH	7 7.03	70	20-1	15	GD	J.King	R.Ffrench	1-3	16f
97	121202	TURNPOLE	6 7.10	74	16-1	6	GD	M.Reveley	L.Charnock	2-6	12,14f
98	311413	SPIRIT OF LOVE	3 8.08	95	11-1	19	GD	M.Johnston	O.Peslier	4-9	11,14,16f
99	2121-41	TOP CEES	9 8.10	95	7-1(SF)	17	GD	I.Balding	K.Fallon	1-2	13f

AGE (wins-runners): 3-Y-O: 2-39, 4-Y-O: 1-96, 5-Y-O: 2-53, **6-Y-O+: 5-80.**

FAVOURITES/SECOND FAVOURITES (strike rate and to a £1 stake): Favs. 9 per cent, -£5. **S.Favs. 21 per cent, +£14.50.**

AVERAGE WINNING RATING: 82.

Introduction

First run in 1839, this is a gruelling test of stamina and only those proven over long-distances need be considered. Look for a horse in the Trainglot, Spirit Of Love or Top Cees mould when making your selection.

Ten year analysis

Age: Winners have come from every age group – although four-year-olds have a weak record – six-year-olds and above boasting the best strike rate.

Weight/Rating: There is no real pattern to the weight or ratings, with horses winning from both ends of the handicap.

Form: Nine won during their preparation, six landing a handicap over at least two miles from July. However, it is equally important to note that six had a maximum of four previous outings. This is a race for fresh horses.

Latest start: Nine had their latest start from September onward, three winning and four making the frame in a handicap.

Betting: Favourites have a poor record, but second favourites have yielded a handsome level-stakes profit since 1990.

Top trainer: Mary Reveley is not one to chase a big prize without reason, and has sent out two winners and one placed horse over the past decade.

NEWMARKET, SATURDAY OCTOBER 14
DEWHURST STAKES (GROUP 1) TWO-YEAR-OLD COLTS AND FILLIES (7f)

YR	FORM	WINNER	WT	S.P.	DRAW	GOING	TRAINER	JOCKEY	FORM IN YEAR WN-RN	WN DIST
90	12301	GENEROUS	9.00	50-1	7	GD	P.Cole	T.Quinn	2-5	5,8f
91	12112	DR DEVIOUS	9.00	3-1F	8	GD-FM	P.Chapple-Hyam	W.Carson	3-5	6,7f
92	111	ZAFONIC	9.00	10-11F	1	GD-FM	A.Fabre(FR)	Pat Eddery	3-3	6,6.5,7f
93	131	GRAND LODGE	9.00	9-4F	1	GD-SFT	W.Jarvis	Pat Eddery	2-3	6,7f
94	111	PENNEKAMP	9.00	5-2JF	5	GD-FM	A.Fabre(FR)	T.Jarnet	3-3	6,7f
95	1111	ALHAARTH	9.00	4-7F	1	GD-FM	W.Hern	W.Carson	4-4	7f
96	1323	IN COMMAND	9.00	10-1	2	GD	B.Hills	M.Hills	1-4	6f
97	1121	XAAR	9.00	11-8F	1	GD	A.Fabre(FR)	O.Peslier	3-4	6,7f
98	110	MUJAHID	9.00	25-1	3	GD	J.Dunlop	R.Hills	2-3	6f
99	11	DISTANT MUSIC	9.00	4-6F	2	GD	B.Hills	M.Hills	2-2	7f

FAVOURITES/SECOND FAVOURITES (strike rate and to a £1 stake): **Favs. 54 per cent, +£5.26.** S.Favs. 0 per cent, -£10.
TOP TRAINER (wins-runners, strike rate and to a £1 stake): **Andre Fabre (3-4, 75 per cent, +£3.78).**

Introduction

This race usually decides the juvenile championship and, while several recent winners became disappointing, Generous, Dr Devious, Zafonic and Pennekamp all went on to win a Classic.

Ten year analysis

Form: Nine had three-five runs beforehand, only two making their debut before June or finishing unplaced. Nine won at least twice, eight scoring over seven furlongs or a mile from August onward.

Latest start: Seven had their latest start over seven furlongs from September, five winning a Group One or Two event.

Best trial: There are no outstanding trials, although it is worth noting that all three of Andre Fabre's winners landed the Group One Prix de la Salamandre.

Betting: Favourites have an excellent record, boasting a 54 per cent strike rate and healthy level-stakes profit. That said, shocks do occur, both Generous (50/1) and Mujahid (25/1) rescuing the bookmakers.

Top trainers: Barry Hills has a useful record (two winners and two placed), but this is Andre Fabre's race. The French maestro has sent out three winners from just four runners since 1990 and his raiders cannot be ignored.

NEWMARKET, SATURDAY OCTOBER 14
CHAMPION STAKES (GROUP 1) (1m 2f)

YR	FORM	WINNER	AGE-WT	RATING	S.P.	DRAW	GOING	TRAINER	JOCKEY	FORM IN YEAR WN-RN	WN DIST
90	114130	**IN THE GROOVE**	3 8.09	-	9-2(SF)	2	GD	D.Elsworth	S.Cauthen	3-8	8,10f
91	1-24311	**TEL QUEL**	3 8.12	-	16-1	12	GD-FM	A.Fabre(FR)	T.Jarnet	2-5	9,10f
92	411041	**RODRIGO DE TRIANO**	3 8.12	-	11-8F	7	GD-FM	P.Chapple-Hyam	L.Piggott	3-6	8,10f
93	11-1441	**HATOOF**	4 9.00	-	5-2F	1	GD	C.Head(FR)	W.Swinburn	2-4	8,10f
94	30-0031	**DERNIER EMPEREUR**	4 9.04	-	8-1	2	GD-FM	A.Fabre(FR)	S.Guillot	1-4	10f
95	1-1102	**SPECTRUM**	3 8.10	119	5-1	1	GD-FM	P.Chapple-Hyam	J.Reid	2-4	8f
96	11-112	**BOSRA SHAM**	3 8.08	128	9-4(SF)	4	GD	H.Cecil	Pat Eddery	2-3	7,8f
97	321212	**PILSUDSKI**	5 9.02	135	EV F	1	GD	Sir M.Stoute	M.Kinane	2-6	10f
98	311-112	**ALBORADA**	3 8.08	118	8-1	5	GD	Sir M.Prescott	G.Duffield	2-3	10f
99	1/1121-0	**ALBORADA**	4 8.13	121	5-1	10	GD	Sir M.Prescott	G.Duffield	0-1	

AGE (wins-runners): **3-Y-O: 6-52,** 4-Y-O: 3-29, 5-Y-O: 1-14, 6-Y-O+: 0-3.
FAVOURITES/SECOND FAVOURITES (strike rate and to a £1 stake): **Favs. 30 per cent, -£2.13.** S.Favs. 18 per cent, -£2.25.
AVERAGE WINNING RATING: 124.

Introduction

The highlight of Champions Day, this race seldom falls to anything other than an outstanding performer and has been particularly kind to fillies over the years. The girls have put the boys into the shade five times since 1990 and are always to be feared.

Ten year analysis

Age: Three and four-year-olds have dominated this race and older horses are best opposed.

Form: There is one vital form pointer – seven won a Group race around ten furlongs from August onward. Ignore that clue at your peril. Fillies have scored 12 times in the last 20 years and must be treated with the utmost respect. As far as the Champion Stakes is concerned, the female of the species is certainly deadlier than the male.

Latest start: All ten ran in a Group race on their latest start, eight from September.

Betting: While there has only been one surprise winner since 1990 – Tel Quel (16/1) – neither favourites nor second favourites have managed to produce a level-stakes profit.

Top trainers: Courtesy of Alborada, Sir Mark Prescott has won the last two renewals. It is also worth noting that French-trained runners have a decent record, winning three times since 1990 and seven times over the past 20 years. Keep an eye on those Gallic raiders.

NEWMARKET, SATURDAY OCTOBER 14
ROCKFEL STAKES (GROUP 3) TWO-YEAR-OLD FILLLIES (7f)

YR	FORM	WINNER	WT	S.P.	DRAW	GOING	TRAINER	JOCKEY	FORM IN YEAR WN-RN	WN DIST
90	21	**CRYSTAL GAZING**	8.08	5-6F	4	GD	L.Cumani	L.Dettori	1-2	6f
91	1111	**MUSICALE**	8.11	7-4F	1	GD-FM	H.Cecil	Pat Eddery	4-4	6,7f
92	31	**YAWL**	8.08	9-4(SF)	7	GD-FM	B.Hills	D.Holland	1-2	7f
93	414	**RELATIVELY SPECIAL**	8.08	11-8F	8	GD-SFT	L.Cumani	R.Cochrane	1-3	6f

94	3332	**GERMANE**	8.08	5-1(SF)	3	GD-FM	M.Bell	M.Fenton	0-4	
95	110	**BINT SALSABIL**	8.12	15-2	7	GD-FM	J.Dunlop	W.Carson	2-3	6,7f
96	1122	**MOONLIGHT PARADISE**	8.12	11-8F	3	GD	S.Bin Suroor	L.Dettori	2-4	6f
97	211	**NAME OF LOVE**	8.12	9-4F	5	GD	D.Loder	K.Fallon	2-3	7f
98	03103	**HULA ANGEL**	8.09	10-1	5	GD	B.Hills	M.Hills	1-5	7f
99	1	**LAHAN**	8.09	7-2JF	1	GD	J.Gosden	R.Hills	1-1	7f

FAVOURITES/SECOND FAVOURITES (strike rate and to a £1 stake): **Favs. 54 per cent, +£6.07**. S.Favs. 20 per cent, -£0.75

Introduction

With the exception of Hula Angel, recent winners of this race have not trained on particularly well. That disappointing pattern may continue.

Ten year analysis

Weight/Rating: Musicale, Bint Salsabil, Moonlight Paradise and Name Of Love have all carried penalties successfully.

Form: Eight had a two-four race preparation, only one making her debut before June. Nine had already scored and maidens should be opposed.

Latest start: Eight ran in a Group or Listed race on their latest start, five winning and two making the frame.

Best trial: Four ran in the Listed Oh So Sharp Stakes (run at Newmarket on September 30), Yawl and Name Of Love winning, while Germane and Hula Angel made the frame.

Betting: Favourites boast a smart 54 per cent strike rate and level-stakes profit.

Top trainer: Barry Hills is an excellent trainer of fillies. His nine runners since 1990 have yielded two wins and four places.

DONCASTER, SATURDAY OCTOBER 21
RACING POST TROPHY (GROUP 1) TWO-YEAR-OLD COLTS AND FILLIES (1m)

YR	FORM	WINNER	WT	S.P.	DRAW	GOING	TRAINER	JOCKEY	FORM IN YEAR WN-RN	WN DIST.
90	11	**PETER DAVIES**	9.00	2-1JF	4	SFT	H.Cecil	S.Cauthen	2-2	7f
91	1213	**SEATTLE RHYME**	9.00	2-1F	7	GD	D.Elsworth	C.Asmussen	2-4	6,8f
92	1	**ARMIGER**	9.00	5-4F	4	SFT	H.Cecil	Pat Eddery	1-1	8f

93	011	**KING'S THEATRE**	9.00	9-2	3	GD	H.Cecil	W.Ryan	2-3	8f
94	11	**CELTIC SWING**	9.00	EV F	5	GD-SFT	Lady Herries	K.Darley	2-2	7f
95	3111	**BEAUCHAMP KING**	9.00	11-4(SF)	3	GD-FM	J.Dunlop	J.Reid	3-4	7,8f
96	2110	**MEDAALY**	9.00	14-1	6	GD	S.Bin Suroor	G.Hind	2-4	7,8f
97	312131	**SARATOGA SPRINGS**	9.00	9-2(SF)	4	GD	A.O'Brien(IR)	M.Kinane	3-6	7,8f
98	12	**COMMANDER COLLINS**	9.00	2-1F	4	HVY	P.Chapple-Hyam	J.Fortune	1-2	7f
99	1	**ARISTOTLE**	9.00	10-1	8	SFT	A.O'Brien(IR)	G.Duffield	1-1	7f

FAVOURITES/SECOND FAVOURITES (strike rate and to a £1 stake): **Favs. 45 per cent, +£2.25.** S.Favs. 18 per cent, -£1.75.
TOP TRAINER (wins-runners, strike rate and to a £1 stake): **Henry Cecil (3-7, 43 per cent, +£3.75).**

Introduction

Run a touch late in the season, this race has a mixed record. While King's Theatre and Celtic Swing trained on into top-class three-year-olds, Peter Davies, Armiger, Beauchamp King, Medaaly and Commander Collins were disappointing.

Ten year analysis

Form: Only one ran more than four times, all ten winning, six over a mile and four at seven furlongs. Avoid those taking a big step-up in trip. Six ran in Group or Listed races, three scoring and two making the frame.

Latest start: Nine had their latest start over seven furlongs or a mile from September, six winning.

Betting: Favourites have a 45 per cent strike rate and small level-stakes profit. While there have been surprise results – Medaaly (14/1) and Aristotle (10/1) – the market is usually a fair guide.

Top trainers: Henry Cecil has the best ten-season record, sending out three winners and a placed horse from just seven runners since 1990. However, it is worth noting that Aidan O'Brien has snared two of the last three runnings. The young master of Ballydoyle has obviously taken a liking to this event.

DONCASTER, SATURDAY NOVEMBER 4
NOVEMBER HANDICAP (1m 4f)

YR	FORM	WINNER	AGE-WT	RATING	S.P.	DRAW	GOING	TRAINER	JOCKEY	FORM IN YEAR WN-RN	WN DIST.
90	141-001	**AZZAAM**	3 9.08	99	7-1(SF)	14	GD-SFT	J.Dunlop	W.Carson	1-3	10f
91	311134	**HIEROGLYPHIC**	3 8.13	91	11-4F	21	GD-SFT	J.Gosden	W.Carson	3-6	12f
92	104241	**TURGENEV**	3 9.00	91	10-1	21	GD	J.Gosden	D.Holland	2-8	10,12f

93	100332	**QUICK RANSOM**	5 8.10	90	6-1F	9	GD	M.Johnston	J.Weaver	1-7	14f
94	041214	**SAXON MAID**	3 8.09	90	16-1	20	HVY	L.Cumani	J.Weaver	2-7	12f
95	0-00111	**SNOW PRINCESS**	3 8.02	73	5-1F	10	GD-FM	Ld Huntingdon	R.Hills	3-5	10.5, 12f
96	033114	**CLIFTON FOX**	4 8.10	96	9-1	14	SFT	J.Glover	N.Day	3-11	9,10f
97	-4021	**SABADILLA**	3 7.08	84	10-1	10	SFT	J.Gosden	R.Ffrench	1-4	12f
98	222312	**YAVANA'S PACE**	6 9.10	105	8-1(SF)	12	SFT	M.Johnston	D.Holland	3-10	10.12f
99	221102	**FLOSSY**	3 7.07	82	5-1(SF)	10	SFT	C.Thornton	A.Beech	5-13	10,12f

AGE (wins-runners): **3-Y-O:** 7-65, 4-Y-O: 1-80, 5-Y-O: 1-39, 6-Y-O+: 1-39.
FAVOURITES/SECOND FAVOURITES (strike rate and to a £1 stake): **Favs. 30 per cent, +£6.75.** S.Favs. 20 per cent, +£8.
AVERAGE WINNING RATING: 90.
TOP TRAINER (wins-runners, strike rate and to a £1 stake): **John Gosden (3-12, 25 per cent, +£13.75).**

Introduction

The last big Flat race of the domestic season, this regularly falls to a smart performer. Hieroglyphic, Quick Ransom, Saxon Maid, Sabadilla and Yavana's Pace were class acts.

Ten year analysis

Age: This is best left to three-year-olds. The youngsters have won seven of the ten renewals since 1990.

Weight/Rating: This is tough to win under a big weight. Only one of the last ten (Yavana's Pace, rated 105) carried more than 9st.

Draw: It is interesting to note that those drawn low have a poor record. All the winners since 1990 came from stalls nine or above.

Form: All ten scored beforehand (seven at least twice), eight winning from August onward. As the average number of previous outings stands at 7.4, there is no truth in the rumour that this is best left to fresh horses.

Latest start: Seven had their latest start in a handicap from October, three winning and four making the frame.

Betting: Favourites and second favourites have produced a level-stakes profit since 1990. The market is a surprisingly useful guide.

Top trainer: Mark Johnston has sent out a couple of well-backed winners, but John Gosden is the leading handler. Manton's new incumbent has sent out three winners and two placed horses from a dozen runners since 1990.